The
Handbook for
Family Cruising

Also by David and Joan Hay

Cruising in Strange Waters
The Downs from the Sea
East Anglia from the Sea
Hilltop Villages of the Chilterns
No Star at the Pole
The Solent from the Sea
The Trees are Full of Song
The West Country from the Sea

The Handbook for Family Cruising

David and Joan Hay

Paul Elek London

Published in Great Britain 1977
by Elek Books Limited
54–58 Caledonian Road London N1 9RN

ISBN 0 236 40103 3

Typeset by Computacomp (UK) Ltd.,
Fort William, Scotland
Printed in Great Britain by
The Anchor Press Ltd.
Tiptree, Essex

Contents

Acknowledgments

If you also travel the seas in a small boat for fun, you will have been surprised and delighted by the friendliness of chance companions in strange harbours. But this is nothing to the kindly help and encouragement you get from complete strangers when you start writing books about the sea and ask for help with the necessary research. When writing this present book, we were especially grateful to Miss Jill Pipe of Fairways Yacht Charters Ltd., Mr C.L. Perkins, South Cornwall Yacht Charter, Captain R.D. Franks, R.N. Retd. of Westoe Boats, Mr D.R. Howard of the Yacht Charter Association Ltd. and Sea Ventures Ltd., and to Sandra Dunningham of the Stourwell Haven Yacht Charters and to the Anvil Yacht Charter firm; to Mr James Hoseason of Hoseasons, Lowestoft and Mr T.E. Howes of Blakes, Wroxham; to a number of sailing schools and especially Captain A. Smith, the Hamble School of Sailing, Mrs B.W. Poole, Scimitar Sailing (Hamble) Ltd. and Commander D.N.A. Cox of the Southern Sailing School; to the Island Cruising Club, Salcombe; for information on yacht mortgages to Commander D.F. Johnson of Hill, Samuel & Co. Ltd., and among the boat designers and builders to Fairways Marine, David Hillyard, Tom Lack Catamarans and Sandwich Yacht Construction Ltd.

For our illustrations we are grateful as usual to our old friend Dennis Mallet for his delightful cartoons, to Mr Tom Lack for permission to reproduce plan and photograph of catamaran interiors, to my godson Sean Gardner for the professional plans of yacht layouts and to Stephen Green for the drawings of typical boats. As usual, we are grateful to the Cruising Association for allowing the reproduction of some cartoons that appeared first in their periodical.

This book is the result of many years cruising with family and friends. We have shared countless good moments with them and now and again there have been bad ones too. They have all contributed something to the ideas we are trying to pass on here and we are grateful for their forbearance and understanding when things have gone wrong and for their cheerful companionship during the many long spells when everything has gone well.

The publishers wish to thank Blakes of Wroxham, Norfolk, England for the use of their picture on the front cover.

List of Illustrations

Introduction

Whether you listen to the talk round the bar at any yacht club, or read the books already published on sailing, you cannot escape the impression that cruising merely consists of learning how to get safely from A to B and how to deal with the basic technical problems of sailing, anchoring and coping with recalcitrant engines. *Nothing, as you will soon learn, if you are thinking of taking up sailing, is further from the truth.*

What the books skate round, or even funk mentioning, and what the 'bar proppers' conveniently forget, is that far more basic and complicated human problem of how you ensure that a family which may contain three generations or that a collection of strangers is going to exist reasonably harmoniously in a demanding and totally strange environment. For the newcomer to the sea, it is not funny to be herded all unprepared into a little wooden or plastic box, which is then turned on its side and well shaken up. It is not only the very young who need mental preparation for this. Perhaps all can benefit from the stimulus of a glimpse of the excitements and pleasures waiting for them in the quiet estuary or strange port at the end of the day.

We are all made differently — thank goodness — and we need a little encouragement to bring out our best qualities. Nowhere else are these needed so much as at sea. The hesitant intellectual may find, with encouragement from an experienced and understanding skipper, that he positively enjoys the rough and tumble of sail changing on the foredeck in a blow, if shown how to do it and not shouted at; many a young man looking wildly for the lee side has been saved from seasickness by an observant elder handing over the tiller abruptly and giving him something practical upon which to concentrate his mind. If you can find time to explain to the very young what is going on and why the boat has taken on a 35° list on a very uneven surface and why you

" ... If she is reluctant it is probably your own fault"

are doing various curious things, they will cease being bored or frightened and take an interest in the proceedings. Tell a child to shut up and he will howl louder, but give him an official position — in charge of stowing and sorting the warps, or bar steward, or tending sheet winches — and he will blossom as a responsible member of the crew.

And what of the most important member of the crew (skipper perhaps apart), I mean the reluctant wife!

If she is reluctant it is probably your own fault. How often does she start her holidays afloat by being shown, casually, a sordid little corner called the galley and told, 'That's where you do your cooking, dear, now we're afloat.' No wonder, feeling slightly seasick, she tells the embryo skipper what he can do with his dream boat and smelly little gas cooker!

If only he had said, instead, 'Sweetie, come and have a break from household chores and suburban traffic and we'll potter up and down a quiet estuary, to begin with. I'll do the cooking for a change and you can try your hand at the tiller and a spot of simple navigation which you'll find far easier than fiddling the housekeeping accounts … !'

Well, who knows? At the end of the week she might even have insisted on doing the cooking — as it should be done — and found plenty of time to enjoy a stretch at the tiller or the fascinating gadgets lying on the chart table when they eventually put to sea for the first short easy passages in fine weather.

I shall always remember a young man who asked, many years ago, if he could join us for a week's cruising down the Normandy coast. I knew he was an experienced sailor, so I asked why he particularly wanted to come on this trip.

'Well,' he said a bit self consciously, 'I am buying a boat and the wife and young family want to join in. I thought I'd better come and see how you run a "floating home" so that they will enjoy themselves and want to cruise again each summer for the fun of it.'

During the years that followed we discovered that there were a considerable number of these rather sensible young men — most of whom were too shy to ask publicly for help or had no one suitable to turn to.

We all talk about this problem and reluctantly come to the conclusion that no sail training curriculum can be made to cover it effectively as it is such a personal matter and varies with each crew. Neither do existing books face up to it. Even the best ones bypass all the human problems of how to adjust the length of passages and choice of weather to the strength and capacity of their crews. For weather is the great imponderable. You cannot control it so you have to adapt yourself and your crew members to it gradually until their experience grows and they become capable of coping with bigger and better waves and the cold and discomforts of night passages. The worst mistake most books make is to treat the woman, whether she be wife or girl friend, as a second-rate being, which in this day and age of women's lib is, to say the least, tactless and at worst fails to establish the fact that she is, together with the skipper, a key member of the crew.

So we are writing this book in the hope that it will fill just this gap in the books on your shelf and be of use, not only to beginners with their first family boat, but also to

4

old hands who are perhaps even more aware through experience of the importance of the very human problems of living afloat. There are already many books on the actual art of sailing or navigating so we will merely indicate what you need to learn and how to go about learning it. Our main purpose is to help you to live safely and enjoyably in a yacht and to decide whether this is the life for you and your family, rather than, say, caravanning.

Cruising is really a way of life rather than a sport — that is more for the racing fraternity. But it is made up, as later chapters indicate, of an almost infinite variety of possibilities and caters equally for the estuary potterer on sunny days and for the more adventurous, for whom there are such delights as the Danish Islands, which hover on the threshold of true fairyland, or the creeks and little harbours of Brittany with their congenial pubs and delicious seafood restaurants.

These, as well as the other delights open to the family when you have mastered the art of living naturally and comfortably in your new environment, are set out in later chapters. There is also a link with the past; you are issued with the same ration books, when granted bonded stores, as those the Elizabethan sailors had and you still get the same thrill as they did when you sail your own little boat into Copenhagen or a Channel port for the first time. Indeed, I think it is only the lone yachtsman on watch at night who can envisage the round world in its primeval entirety. True, he can only see a small part of the curve but he will be a dull dog who doesn't feel that the rest of it is now separated from him only by a bit more water.

Part 1

An Easy Start on Inland Waterways

There may be a few rash characters whose initial enthusiasm for the sailing idea is great enough to entice them into buying a boat and going straight off across the Channel or North Sea. If they are lucky they may even get away with it without having to summon the lifeboat to get them out of trouble. Most of us, however, are more cautious in our approach to a new idea that may have dropped like a bombshell into the family councils and the first tentative suggestion will be the prelude to weeks or months of family discussions, arguments and hesitations. Not the least of the worries, in these days of financial stringency, will be the thought of heavy expenditure on a project that might in the end prove a failure. For in the early stages, the purchase of a boat and the essential equipment is going to be a drain on resources, even if in the long run it turns out to be a most economical way of giving the family wonderful holidays.

So, most families will want some sort of trial run before committing themselves and if this trial run is to succeed it is important that it should not be too ambitious. Initially there are two separate things to master:

The art of managing a boat   *and*

The art of living afloat.

Some members of the family may get so enthusiastic about learning to sail that they won't mind a few discomforts; for others the whole holiday may be spoilt if the domestic side is a shambles. It will depend a little on the members of your family, but for many we suggest that the gentlest of introductions may be the best — a week or so on inland waterways. What is more, in these sheltered waters you can do this *in a hired boat* even though you are a beginner, so you needn't commit yourselves to any greater expenditure than the normal annual holiday.

There are three main possibilities to choose from: the Broads, the Thames, and the Canal network. For each of them you will find the names of hirers in any of the yachting magazines, but to get an overall idea of possibilities it would be worth getting brochures first from the two big Norfolk firms, Blakes of Wroxham and Hoseasons of Lowestoft, because both firms charter boats not only over the whole range of English inland waterways but also include the Caledonian canal, the river Shannon and some French canals for good measure.

If you are insistent that the trial should include some experience of actual sailing, then you really have no alternative to the Broads — and that of course is why they are so popular. The beginner who wants to sail will be given some free instruction by the charter firm, but might find it easier early or late in the season, before there are too many other boats about.

We ourselves took our first little boat to the Broads for sailing trials one Easter, but our first real cruise was on the Thames and this is as good a place as any to start to learn the art of living afloat — and the cruise won't be uneventful either.

When the boatyard representative has shown you round and explained the working of the engine, the toilet, the cooker and any other vital pieces of equipment, it is very tempting just to dump all your gear and provisions on the floor and push off. My advice is, don't. Even in your own boat, where you know where everything should be stowed, it may take an hour or more to unpack and in a strange boat it is bound to take longer. What is more, if you are unused to cruising, it will be a miracle if you haven't taken far too many clothes for the available lockers, and it is no bad thing to discover this while you can still take the surplus back to the car. There is nothing more irritating after a day or two than having the cabin littered with items for which you cannot find a home.

Managing a boat

When you have unpacked, you will be shown how to manage the boat, but even after this I hope you won't rush off too quickly to the first lock without a few experiments in handling the boat on your own, for there are several things that will at first seem rather strange. First, you are in a moving vehicle that has no brakes — the best way of stopping is to slow down in plenty of time and judge your speed so accurately that you will just glide to a halt at the right place. The alternative is to put the engine in reverse — assuming you have a reverse — and the only other way (in desperation) is to get a rope round a post, if you can, and hold on.

In trying to achieve any of these you discover the next two problems, that the water itself may be moving and that your boat is far more affected by wind than any road vehicle. Indeed, with wind and tide or current behind you it is difficult to stop, even by going into reverse, so that where possible you turn head to wind and tide to slow you down. On inland waterways of course, this is not always possible when waiting for a lock to open.

Thirdly, a boat will turn more easily than any car because it pivots on its centre point — this has both advantages and disadvantages. Fourth, the direction in which you move isn't determined by the way you point the bows but by the action of the water on the rudder, which pushes the stern round. This isn't as obvious with wheel steering on a motor boat as with tiller steering on many sailing boats, but it is no bad thing to get into the habit from the beginning of thinking what the rudder is doing. And it does matter when you go into reverse because then the action of the water on the rudder works the other way and you have to reverse the steering.

Finally, boats are an awkward shape for bringing alongside a straight bank or wall because the side of a boat is not straight, it has a bulge in the middle — a sort of middle-aged spread. The difficulty is that unless there is somebody ashore to whom you can throw a warp as you come in, the crew on the foredeck may need to grab a chain, or a ladder, or a post quickly, to help stop the boat and probably get ashore as well. But if you push the bow in to help the foredeck crew, the stern will swing out, while if you go in so that you lie nicely alongside, the bow may be too far away for the crew to reach anything. If there are two or three crew, so that one can concentrate on fending off and another on tying up, it is not too difficult, but a two-man crew, one in the bows and the other steering, will have to move fast to come alongside neatly.

A trip up the Thames

Lock drill
This simple explanation may be enough to show why a trial run or two up and down a straight part of the river may be desirable before tackling the first lock, where you meet all the problems of stopping and coming alongside without damaging your own or other boats. Those living near enough to any navigable inland waterway, whether river or canal, may find it worth making a trip there a week or so before the cruise to watch boats going through a lock. Some, you will notice, come in so quietly and easily that it looks no more difficult than parking a car alongside the pavement. On other boats there will be a great flurry of activity, with people rushing about the decks and a stream of shouted orders from the cockpit, orders which rise to a crescendo as the boat comes in too fast, bumps the lock walls, bounces off and has to be fended off by the other boats before it does any damage. Fortunately the lock keepers are very kind and patient and most boat owners helpful to anyone in trouble, so eventually somebody gets warps ashore and the boat tied

up so that the lock, when full of boats, can be filled or emptied. When the gates open again, with luck the offending boat will go out rather more smoothly than it came in, but there really would have been no need for all the schemozzle if the skipper had thought of briefing his crew properly in advance, and given them time to get ready.

One of the problems is that it is difficult for anyone experienced to understand how lost the beginner may feel for the first two or three days afloat. Things are called by curious names and an apparently simple instruction is more likely to be met by a look of blank bewilderment than by instant action. So it is just no good saying as the lock comes into sight 'Fix those fenders on the port side.' The crew may need to work out which is the port side, may look round helplessly to discover what a fender is, and anyhow won't have any idea where to attach it. Then, before that job is finished, you find you are in the lock, with more instructions about getting a warp ashore when there's no obvious means of doing so — assuming even that they remember that a warp is a rope which, by now, should have been attached somewhere on the foredeck. Tempers begin to get a bit frayed and the cruise isn't off to a good start, particularly as the skipper is much more worried than he will admit about coping with a strange boat and rather sensitive about the bad impression he and his crew are making.

This is not to say, incidentally, that even the most experienced don't now and again have troubles in locks. As we have just explained, keeping control, while going slowly with a strong wind up your tail and swirls coming in from the weir next door, will demand good judgment, smart crew work and a spot of luck, so don't worry if things go wrong now and then — it happens to all of us. Anyhow, after a few locks, the family will have got their lock drill wrapped up and be beginning to enjoy themselves. The great thing about the inland waterways, and one thing that makes them an ideal start for a young family is that there are jobs for everybody — even a four year old can flip a fender overboard, as long as you first tie on both the fender and the youngster!

Mooring for the night
After a few more locks the sight of other boats tying up reminds you that it will soon be time for you too to get settled for the night. Even if you wanted to go on after dark, you could not because the locks close. Theoretically you should be able to moor up against the bank anywhere on the towpath side of a river, but you will soon discover that the choice of the actual site gives scope for as many family arguments as the choice of any other picnic spot. The first likely place is condemned because there are already two other boats there; the next because there are cows around and one of the children doesn't like them; a third stretch looks possible but you cannot get close enough to the bank — it is too shallow and there is a temporary alarm when you find you have gone aground — fortunately the boathook just reaches the bank and a vigorous push combined with the engine in reverse generally gets you off. Round the next bend you come into a delightful reach where, from the towpath, you look onto a lovely wooded island. It looks just right and there's no one there so you get ashore, hammer in a couple of pitons and tie up. Everything seems wonderful

until another boat comes along rather fast and you are rocked about violently. You look at each other in dismay until somebody realises that you're in a narrow reach where the wash from passing boats will be worse than usual. Reluctantly you pull out the pitons and push off again. Soon the river widens. There is one boat tied up at the beginning of the reach but there is plenty of room to get well away further along and at least the family agrees by now that no one wants to go any further.

I'm sure you will have brought with you a meal prepared at home so that you can enjoy this first evening without having to cook. In any case you will have had enough excitements for one day without adding to them the problems of cooking in a ship's galley, which we discuss in Part 4. You may have travelled no more than ten miles, and it is less than a day since you started your holiday, but already home will seem very distant as you sit in the cockpit and watch the evening lights on the water. Somebody yawns and there is a general move towards bed, until arguments from the children in the forecabin warn you that in a congested space it is slightly easier if they don't both try to undress at the same time. It will take a day or so before you shake down into some sort of routine.

The Thames Scene

The Thames takes you through some lovely country and some attractive little towns like Marlow, Henley and Sonning. There are public landing stages where you can tie up for a time if you want to go ashore and the riverside pubs have their own private stages to entice you in for a glass of beer. At first your progress may seem rather slow, but you will soon get used to travelling at little more than walking speed. Inevitably these middle reaches from about Staines to Oxford are popular and at the height of the season progress will be even slower because of queues at locks, but this perhaps is all to the good — one of the first lessons to learn about living afloat is that you should *never* be in a hurry — unless you are trying to beat the weather and reach sanctuary before a gale hits you. At least that won't apply on inland waterways, where you can always pull in and tie up if conditions get unpleasant. Incidentally if you want to find the most peaceful stretch, you might like to try the 32 miles between Oxford and Lechlade. Once clear of Oxford you hardly go through a village, let alone a town, though there are still riverside pubs like the Rose Revived, the Trout Inn and the Anchor Inn near Buscot to entice you to make the most of your leisurely life. In these upper reaches the banks are covered with wild flowers and you seem to be in the middle of your own private garden as purple loosestrife, meadow sweet, foxgloves, ox-eye daisies and a host of others peep in through the portholes.

The canals

Much of what we have written about the Thames applies equally to the canals, except for one big difference. Here there are no friendly lock keepers to help and do all the work — you are just given a handle and have to work the machinery yourself and jolly hard work it can be too. Though on the Thames you can keep a crew of three or four fully employed, two can manage perfectly well if they have to; on the canals three is really the minimum and it is better to have more. It is the ideal holiday if your family consists of a number of active and energetic young men from the age of about ten upwards, but, equally, I've known a party of old age pensioners enjoy a canal cruise provided there were enough of them.

There are various possibilities, details of which, together with a list of the boat hirers in the area, can be found in *The Canals Book* (see bibliography).

This gives a fascinating insight into the number still working, and they are so well scattered round the country that anyone who wants to try them out can arrange a weekend cruise near home, without even giving up any leave. Most of the canals are connected in a single network within which England and Wales can be explored from the Fens or the Trent valley across to the Welsh mountains and from the river Wey in Surrey to the great waterway over the Pennines which connects Leeds and Liverpool. The canals take you through unknown country and even industrial towns take on a new interest when seen from the water rather than the road. For those who want to see further afield, the Caledonian canal in Scotland and the River Shannon in Ireland have much to offer.

Part 2

Preparing for Tidal Waters

If the first gentle cruise on inland waterways has been a failure, your dream of owning a boat may already be vanishing. But if the family has enjoyed itself, it will probably be enthusiastic to try something a little more ambitious the following year and venture into tidal waters. This time it will not just be a question of hiring a boat light-heartedly and learning as you go. Cruising in tidal waters is very different. On inland waterways it is difficult to run into real trouble, unless you ignore all warning notices and get swept down a weir, whereas out at sea it is all too easy for things to go wrong if you don't know what you are doing. It is no good thinking of cruising unless you are prepared to do quite a lot of preparatory work to learn the essentials that you will need before going out to sea as skipper of a small boat.

The problems of living aboard under conditions very different from those on the Thames will be discussed in

Part 4. Here we are first going to outline what you need to know and how you can acquire the necessary knowledge and experience. As we have already said, this is not a technical book, so you won't find all the answers here; but we hope to tell you where to find most of them.

How much you need to learn will depend to some extent on your own inclinations and particularly on your choice between:

Sail or power

Listening to any sailing enthusiast, one might assume that cruising automatically means cruising under sail. This of course is nonsense, and indeed in America the word 'yacht' applies to what we in England would call a 'motor cruiser', while the English yacht is called a 'sail boat'. In either, you can enjoy the essence of cruising — travelling and exploring along the coast, up and down rivers and across the seas with your home on your back, rather like a snail. A motor cruiser often has more living space, because there is less gear to stow; it may also enable you to go further afield because it tends to be faster and slightly less affected by wind and weather. But it is often more uncomfortable out at sea and inevitably more expensive and noisy. You may even find it a bit dull after a while. There's nothing like the feel of gliding over the waves, or the sound of water swishing against the hull or the fun of sailing into a foreign port after crossing the seas using no power except the wind — which is free, even if it has a frustrating habit of blowing from the wrong direction.

We shall come back to this question of types of boats in

17

A Sheltered Anchorage in Perse Bay on Ullswater. There are many enchanting anchorages like this on inland lakes if your boat is light enough to trail and your range of cruising grounds is enormously extended. There is a list of launching ramps.

Part 5, and at this stage we are assuming that you're thinking of sailing rather than motoring, but before we go on to the problems of sailing we would make two further points.

First, it is not easy to find firms which will charter *motor boats* for coastal cruising. Those that exist will probably advertise in *Motor Boat and Yachting* and they will ask you to show that you have some experience in boat handling — a cruise on inland waterways at least — though they may accept a relative novice who is prepared to take the firm's boatmen out with them until they can demonstrate their own competence.

Heybridge — a Typical East Anglian Sea Lock to the Inner Basin. Here, where Dutch, French and English yachts rub sides, a stone's throw from the pub, you can enjoy the well known continental camaraderie — without even troubling to cross the sea.

Secondly, any modern cruising yacht will have a small auxiliary engine as well as sails and, as we shall see, there are occasions when the 'mechanical top sail', as it is sometimes called, is more than useful. So, whether intending to motor or sail those who are not knowledgeable about engines should include some instruction in their preparation for going to sea. Even up estuaries, let alone out at sea, you may be on your own if anything goes wrong; you cannot just pull into the bank and walk to the nearest telephone to summon assistance. If you cannot cope with basic repairs and maintenance

19

you may have to wait hours for help, even if you are in some danger, and the rescue services, if they find you eventually, are not going to be amused when they discover there is nothing wrong but a choked jet or faulty injector.

Learning to sail

If you are intending to buy your own boat immediately, you can, legally, take possession and push off out to sea even if you have never set foot in a sailing boat before. It sounds ridiculous, but that happens to be the law. Fortunately, few people are so foolhardy as to risk their own safety and that of their precious new boat in this way, and at the least you should be able to find a friend with enough experience to come with you, or take you out in his own boat, in order to 'show you the ropes'.

Chartering yachts

There are plenty of firms chartering cruising yachts if you are not ready to buy yet, but first you will have to get adequate experience. How much experience they demand varies a little between firms and they may impose conditions on those whose only experience is in dinghy sailing. One, for example, says that he would give such applicants his smallest boat and insist that they didn't go out of the river; another that they should have an instructor aboard for the first day or two to give them a 'conversion course'. Once you can satisfy the charter firm that you are competent, this is an excellent way to start for those who are still uncertain what to do, or just can't afford to buy their own boat. Indeed there are a number

20

of yachtsmen nowadays who charter year after year. It saves them the time and responsibility of maintaining their own boat and enables them to extend their cruising range, by starting from a different home port each year. Those interested have only to look through the advertisement pages of a yachting magazine to find where to write for the brochures.

Books on sailing
But, to return to the basic problem, if you have never sailed at all and have no friends who will take you out in their own boats, how do you set about learning? Well, for a start, I should go straight to the local bookshop or library. There are plenty of books available; two or three new ones teaching beginners how to sail come out each year and we have simply listed in the bibliography a few that we have found helpful.

Initially, you should concentrate on three things in studying these books. First you should learn something about the *theory* of sailing; secondly you should try to master some of the nomenclature and thirdly you could try to work out some of the examples of boat handling for manoeuvres such as anchoring and taking off. Then having read the book once you go back and read it all over again — and a third time if you can. It all helps when you get afloat.

Dinghy sailing
There are some who maintain that dinghy sailing is the only sensible start for beginners, particularly if they are young. While we disagree with the view that it is the *only* way to learn, there is no doubt that it is the quickest and

21

easiest way of getting some practical experience, and helping to develop a judgment of wind speed and direction, the sensitivity to the boat's reactions and the quick thinking that make the good rather than the mediocre helmsman. A dinghy is light and so tender that if you do not spot at once what she is trying to do and counteract it if necessary, you will probably capsize. It won't do you any harm, but it is uncomfortable getting wet! If you have a dinghy club within reach it is well worth going along to see if you can join. You don't need your own boat; you just offer to crew for others to start with.

But, if you cannot get practice in dinghies, there are other alternatives.

Crewing for other owners
This is a common way of getting experience for those with no boat of their own. Indeed, until a few years ago it was the only way apart from dinghy sailing. Often the owners concerned are an elderly couple who need help in managing the boat after the family has grown up and gone away or married and is no longer free to sail. Again, the yachting magazines carry some advertisements; in addition, organisations like the Cruising Association compile annual 'Owners and Crew' lists (not necessarily restricted to members) to bring together owners who need crews and crews who want a boat to sail in. It is normal though not invariable practice with these arrangements to share living expenses, and with the right owners, prepared to take some trouble to teach keen beginners, this can be one of the best ways of learning. The risk is that with a personality clash you might be put

off for life.

The other snag is that though a husband and wife crew will often be welcome, it is rare to find owners prepared to take children if you all want to learn together. You may find, too, that some charter firms are sceptical about your experience unless you have crewed for several years.

Chartering a yacht with professional skipper and/or crew
Though a more expensive way of learning this has attractions in that it enables you to combine a family holiday with learning to sail and navigate. Once again the yachting magazines carry advertisements, and in theory it is up to you as the charterer to say where you want to go, though you may have to be very firm to avoid being taken on a more ambitious cruise than we would advise for a first effort. (See page 31 below.)

Sailing schools
These, a development of the last few years, are perhaps the best of all methods of instruction for those who can afford the time and money. Courses vary in both length and standard, but the most relevant point here is that most schools reckon that, after a five- or six-day beginners' course (average cost about £80 on 1976 prices), many students acquire sufficient skill and knowledge to sail a cruiser and navigate in tidal waters by day. Husband and wife crews are always welcome on these courses, with the exception of honeymoon couples who, one School Principal commented, had better go to a hotel because there would be insufficient privacy! This same Principal advises portly unfit business men in their

23

60s not to try, and suggests they stick to motor cruisers. Many of these schools do not take children — the age limit varies from sixteen to eighteen and in most the students live aboard for the duration of the course. In no other way, it is suggested, can they learn what it is all about — a view with which we would whole-heartedly agree. There is all the difference in the world between day sailing, when you can go home, if wet and cold, to a nice hot bath and having to sort yourselves out in a crowded cabin, trying to prevent wet oilskins dripping over berths and sleeping bags.

Once again, the advertisement pages of yachting magazines provide details. There are a number of these schools nowadays and it is worth writing for several brochures to see which will suit you best. Some schools, incidentally, provide facilities for students to charter their own boats after they have taken a course.

Elementary navigation and pilotage

A charter firm, in considering your application, will also demand evidence that you have learnt sufficient about navigation and pilotage to find your way when out of sight of land and to get back safely into shelter, even if you are returning to a strange harbour with a difficult entrance. It is no good arguing that this won't be necessary because you have no intention of going out of sight of land. Strange things happen at sea and a bank of fog can roll up out of a clear sky. We well remember watching Alderney, with its dangerous rocky coast, disappearing before our eyes as a curtain of fog was drawn slowly across the island, reaching the corner we

'Fog! I know this bit of sea like the back of my hand.' But – you
may not be the only one about!

25

had to turn just before we did. Even more startling was an evening in Harwich harbour when within two minutes everything was blotted out by a thick belt of fog. I have never before had to demand a course from one buoy to another inside a harbour I know backwards, and it was all rather eerie as an old Thames barge loomed up beside us looking like a ghost ship, and, a pilot boat chugged cautiously across our bows.

Whether you are going to sea in a motor boat or a sailing yacht, whether it be your own or a chartered boat, you must know how to find your way and it is quite a daunting experience the first time you realise that the land has disappeared and you are on your own. The sea looks so vast and on a cloudy day when sun or stars are covered, your sense of direction is useless.

If you are going to a sailing school, elementary navigation will be included in the syllabus, but you shouldn't wait until you are afloat before starting to learn. You will make better use of your time afloat by using it to practise than by spending it on the theory and methods, which can be better learnt ashore beforehand.

The syllabus
In outline, what you need to know is:
1. How to use a *Compass* — and this includes making the correct allowance for the inaccuracies of a magnetic compass which does not point due North — the mysteries of variation and deviation when you start to look up your books. Once aboard you may be surprised to find that keeping an accurate compass course while steering is not as easy as it sounds!

2. How to read a *Chart* (available from chart agents or yacht chandlers) which can be described as a sea map showing depths (usually at low water), offshore hazards such as sandbanks, rocks and wrecks with their warning buoys and the coasts with harbours, rivers and significant seamarks such as church towers or conspicuous tall buildings. For the British Isles and adjacent waters there are three series:

    (i) Admiralty Charts — the most detailed but not necessarily the easiest for the beginner to follow.

    (ii) Stanford's Coloured Charts for Coastal Navigation — a graphic and clear presentation of offshore hazards, even if occasionally they make navigation look a little easier than it is.

    (iii) Imray, Laurie, Norie and Wilson yachting charts — equally clear and sometimes a little more detailed.

It is incidentally even more important to have an up to date chart than a current road map and before a cruise any old charts should be sent for correction to one of the chart agents given in Appendix B unless the owner has access to the Admiralty notices which enable him to make his own corrections or, for the Imray, Laurie, Norie and Wilson charts obtains the list published periodically by that firm.

3. How to work out the *Course* using compass and chart and allowing for the effects of tides.

4. The meaning of the different sea marks or *Buoys* which indicate both the navigable channels and hazards such as rocks and sandbanks. Out at sea,

spotting buoys is one vital job all the family can share and it will keep them interested — an important point on a long passage.

Now, six months ago, I could have told you that any book on navigation would give you the information you needed, and that the British system wasn't complicated — the only difficulties came when you 'went foreign' and that wouldn't be for a year or two. But 1977 is to see the beginning of a change to a new, internationally agreed, uniform system of buoyage, a change which will take three years to complete. In 1977 the new system will be introduced in an area east of Dover and up the East Coast to Southwold, while most of the South Coast won't change until the following year and the rest of the British Isles not until 1979. For the next two or three years, therefore, most of us will have to use both systems. What is even more important is to check, when using any book on navigation, that it is up to date. I also suggest that the artist in the family makes a pack of cards, each with a different buoy drawn on one side and details of what it means with the different light and sound signals it emits on the back, so that you can play parlour games and test each other at intervals.

5. How to check the position by taking compass *Bearings*.

6. How to read a harbour plan, including the instructions for what may be a complicated buoyed entrance. These plans are sometimes included on charts and will always be found in the various *Pilot Books* and *Harbour Guides* (see bibliography) for the

relevant part of the coast.

Even with the best instructions, finding your way safely into some harbours is not as easy as it sounds. The various marks and buoys may be difficult to spot if there are many other boats about and you often have little time to think. You can't just draw into the kerb to study the map if you are doubtful, nor will it be easy to turn round if you've gone wrong. You need to learn, therefore, how to visualise the entrance from a plan as well as the meaning of the different marks and signals.

How to learn

It is not difficult to teach yourself navigation at home. Most of the elementary books have adequate chapters on it, in addition to the more specialised volumes, which set appropriate exercises. Alternatively, if you hate teaching yourself you may well find that there is an evening course within your area or that you can take a correspondence course. Whichever you do, please give yourself plenty of time to practise. Working out courses on the large flat stable area of the dining table is easier than in a restricted space in a moving boat and indeed most yachtsmen, when planning a cruise, do as much preparatory work as they can at home.

Rules and regulations

Yachting is a sport, or pastime, or way of life — whichever you like to call it — which is still less regimented than most activities in this latter half of the twentieth century. There is no licence or test certificate, though yachtsmen are increasingly being encouraged to acquire suitable qualifications. There is no compulsory insurance, even third party, though in our view the yachtsman who fails to insure is guilty of criminal negligence.

But we can hardly expect to be entirely free, especially if we want to sail in the congested waters round the British Isles where we, in our little six or eight ton yachts, use the same international waters, the same channels and the same harbours as a supertanker.

The international regulations for preventing collisions at sea

These therefore apply to us (with certain modifications to suit size) just as much as to large boats. We are expected to observe 'the ordinary practice of seamen' and it is a sobering thought that if we should pick up an SOS on our radios and appear to be the boat nearest to the ship in trouble, it is our duty to go and see if we can help until a bigger and better ship arrives on the scene.

It will be obvious therefore that it is the duty of every skipper to know these regulations and to ensure that any member of his crew in charge of a watch understands them as well. They are published in, among other places, *Reed's Nautical Almanac* — a book I'd advise, at least for one year, because it is such a mine of information. Lights, buoys and harbour signals; weather forecasting and meteorology; safety, distress and rescue; distance tables, tide tables, sun and star tables — these are only a few of the subjects covered, not to mention some invaluable ready reckoners for speeding up some of the navigational calculations.

Port entry signals

Sailing into a big harbour always gives us a bit of a thrill, but we do have to appreciate that we in our small boats must often be a nuisance in a busy commercial port and that we will be welcome only if we are meticulous in observing regulations and harbour signals.

Harbours such as Dover and Calais have entrances so narrow that one-way traffic is essential; many have a number of different arms and it is only the Harbour Master, up in his signal tower, who knows what is happening. So, don't believe anyone who tells you that small boats needn't bother with the harbour signals you'll find in Reed's and the Pilot books.

Choosing your cruising area

The day's sail

On a first cruise, particularly if it is of short duration — say two or three weeks — we do urge you not to be too ambitious. Of course you'd love to sail across the Channel, enter some foreign port and come back with a few bottles of 'duty free'. There will be time for that in other years, but to start with, you will feel happier if you stay within sight of land and if your sea passages are not more than a few miles — a four- or five-mile passage is quite enough for a first venture. You need therefore to go to a part of the coast where the harbours or rivers are close together so that you can cruise from one to the other in a series of short day hops.

Even more important, however, is to choose an area where there is plenty of sheltered water in estuaries and up the navigable part of rivers. You need this sheltered water particularly if you are embarking on a family

31

The first time you ignore harbour signals, it may be the quickest passage anybody has had—to the next world!

cruise: first to provide conditions suitable for a beginner to learn and secondly to give the family something to do on days when it isn't possible to go out to sea because the wind is too strong. Even experienced yachtsmen don't set out in a gale or even in a very strong wind if it's blowing in the wrong direction, because there is no point in taking unnecessary risks and you won't make any useful progress against a head wind and rough seas. So, if you are gale-bound in a harbour like Ramsgate, there is nothing for it but to go for walks or to the cinema or swim — not quite what you had hoped for on a cruising holiday, and the gale may well last two or three days, or more — we once had a solid week of them. Even in sheltered waters there may be days when sailing will not be attractive if the gale is accompanied by torrential rain, but more often than not you can have plenty of fun, well reefed down, sailing up rivers on days when you wouldn't dream of going out to sea.

With this in mind therefore we would suggest that there are four areas round the British Isles that would be particularly suitable for a first cruise. They are:

1. The Harwich Estuary on the east coast, with its two rivers, the Orwell and the Stour, a large area of relatively sheltered water in the harbour itself without getting into the big ship channel, and the delightful Walton Backwaters (Arthur Ransome's *Secret Waters*) just round the corner without going out to sea. And, if you're ready after a few days for a coastal cruise, the Deben is only four miles away up coast. Further down coast, the Blackwater and Colne area is another possibility but it is rather more crowded.

2. Poole Harbour, with its twelve miles up to Wareham, the creeks round Brownsea Island and a maze of little channels and islands which would keep anyone happy for days, without going out to sea.

3. Plymouth harbour which, like Harwich, has two rivers, the St Germans and Truro, to explore as well as the spacious harbour area, with a possibility of a short cruise to the Yealm as the highlight of the holiday.

4. Falmouth, with the Fal and the Truro rivers and their creeks, the whole expanse of the harbour and the delightful Helford River only about five miles away. This is perhaps the loveliest and least spoilt of all these areas, but it is a matter of taste and domestic convenience.

A note on charts and pilot books for these areas is included in the bibliography.

With the exception of Poole, all these estuaries have the added advantage that entrance is easy under any conditions, except of course fog.

You will notice that we haven't included the Solent and Chichester harbour among our four suggestions, because in our view this area is much too popular and too crowded for a beginner.

The night's rest: moorings and marinas

We have so far been thinking of the cruising areas in relation to daytime activity. It is, however, equally important to consider the type of resting place you would like when you have finished sailing and want to settle down for the evening, and your final choice may be a compromise.

34

Basically, what you have to decide is whether you're happy to sit on the boat and amuse yourselves when not sailing, or whether everybody is keen to rush ashore at the first opportunity and stretch their legs, or sample the gay life of whatever harbour you are visiting. If your idea of cruising is to find peace and privacy, then you will probably feel happier on a mooring or at anchor where you can only get ashore by dinghy, whereas more social types will prefer a marina where they can just step ashore whatever the conditions. The point is that there will not necessarily be the choice between moorings and marinas in any one area, which is why it is important to bear this in mind when deciding where you want to go. Indeed, it is such an important decision that it is worth going into the alternatives in a little more detail.

Moorings In tidal waters, as you will appreciate, you can only get even a shallow draught boat near the bank at high water, so the rest of the time, if you want to lie afloat, you have to anchor off and get ashore by dinghy. Moorings are really permanent anchorages, laid down originally at places where local fishermen and coasting barges used to lie because they provided the two essentials — shelter from the prevailing wind and good landing, at least at some states of the tide — and in most of these old anchorages there is also a friendly pub. At some stage, someone decided that the sweat of dropping an anchor and pulling it up again was excessive, so they put down something more permanent.

When yachting started to become popular, yachtsmen, like fishermen, wanted somewhere to leave their boats when they had to go back to work, and for them also these old anchorages were the obvious places to lay their own moorings. At first these were few in number, but within the last few years moorings have spread so that they now extend a mile or more up and down the river. This would mean a long row to the landing place, so most dinghies now have a small outboard motor.

Most moorings consist of two fishermen-type anchors, with one fluke sawn off. These are buried deep in the mud and connected by a heavy chain. To this, another length of chain is attached, lighter but strong enough to hold the weight of the boat when it pulls against the mooring. It is by this lighter chain that the boat is moored, but in the older type of moorings, there is also a length of rope attached to the chain and finally a buoy. When picking up a mooring it is the buoy that one catches with the boathook, then you pull all the rope aboard until you reach the chain, and bring enough of that in to lash round a post or winch on the foredeck. NEVER tie up by the rope; it isn't safe. You must go on pulling in until you reach the chain.

Recently, to complicate matters, a different type of mooring has been introduced with a large buoy attached directly to the chain. The buoys are too big to get aboard, so with these you just get a loop of rope through the ring on top of the buoy and bring that aboard. Many of these big buoys have a permanent loop of very thick rope that the owners have put on themselves, just the right length for their own boats.

On a swinging mooring each boat has its own buoy, to which it is attached only by the bow, so that it is free to act naturally and lie head to tide. In other words it swings (turns) every six hours as the tide changes. There is a great sense of freedom in lying at such a mooring, but it does of course require a fair amount of water space for each boat and in the more popular centres such as the Hamble this can no longer be provided. To economise on space a boat is moored fore and aft so that it cannot swing. In some places it is connected to buoys, in others there are two great posts known as trots to which five or six boats can be moored alongside each other. You still need the dinghy to get ashore, but have lost most of the privacy because you are cheek by jowl with other occupied boats.

I remember one night on trots at Cowes we had an enormous Dutch *Hoogaar* next to us. It was as full of children, musical instruments and women with high-pitched saw-edged voices as a Belgian barge is full of dogs. The children yelled and banged drums all night and the women threw cooking pots at each other — or so it seemed to us trying to get some sleep next door. We left at early dawn and cheerfully faced a Force 7 rather than another night of life on a trot. But don't worry — I suspect we were a bit unlucky.

Marinas or Yacht Harbours From the introduction of trots it was only a short step to the modern marina or yacht harbour, designed to squeeze the maximum number of boats into a given space. In the older harbours, if there was room for yachts at all, they either had to anchor or to tie up to a wall, with other yachts tying up alongside each other when there was no wall space left. If you were on the outside you had to climb across all the other boats to get ashore; on the inside you had everyone else tramping across your decks. Life could become quite interesting — as in Jersey one morning, when the Harbour Master untied the inner boat of a whole line to make room for a ferry and, still tied together, they started to drift across the harbour with the occupants fast asleep. At last a head popped up to see what was happening and somebody thought of starting a motor to try to control the flotilla.

But this was the old-style harbour and the modern marina is a much more sophisticated affair, with floating pontoons to which each boat can be tied individually, enabling the occupants to step ashore. In some you tie up by bow or stern, with the other end anchored or attached to a buoy to prevent it wagging about; at others there is a series of neat little finger pontoons alongside which you lie. Some of these marinas are old harbours converted to this modern use; others have been dug out of derelict land, saltings or old mill pools. In all of them a yacht of up to about six feet draught can lie afloat at any state of the tide, but many, which are in tidal waters, have solved the problem of keeping the water in as the tide ebbs by constructing a sill across the entrance. This seems that you cannot get over the sill at certain states of the tide, even where the sill has been replaced by a lock, entry may be restricted to an hour or two before or after high water.

Whenever a new scheme is mooted the word 'marina' tends to provoke an immediate public reaction, the authorities conjuring up pictures of a sophisticated, chromium-plated establishment, full of juke boxes and noisy parties. For most marinas this could not be further from the truth. Many yachtsmen like them because they provide the great convenience of being able to step ashore. They are placed where it is easy to fill up your water and fuel tanks without having to carry heavy cans, and many have electric points on the pontoons. Most have toilets, showers and some sort of chandler's shop where tinned food can be found as well as ship's gear. In many, too, there is by now a club house where visiting yachtsmen are welcome at the bar and in some cases a restaurant. For most yacht harbours, that is about all you will find — you may not even be near a village shop. There will be some social life as yachtsmen visit each other and look at each other's boats, but with a lot of boats at close quarters it is obvious that life is tolerable only if everyone is considerate and late, noisy parties are a rarity.

Inevitably, and particularly because round the British Isles they are mainly built in tidal waters, marinas are expensive to construct and the fees a good deal higher than those on a swinging mooring, but it is all a matter of taste — some yachtsmen prefer the convenience of the marina to the privacy of the swinging mooring.

The home port
If you have decided to charter, you should now be ready to contact firms in the area of your choice. If, however, you are proposing to buy your own yacht at once, you will first have to decide where you want to base it when not in use and in the choice of this 'home port', there will be additional considerations.

With a very small boat you might even decide to keep it at home and trail it to a launching site every time you want a few days afloat. Modern GRP boats are so light that there is no difficulty in either trailing or launching and you can get an *Index of Launching Sites* to tell you where to put it in the water.

Many larger boats are trailed regularly at the beginning and end of each season (if there is room to park them in the garden) to save the cost of winter lay-up. There are a few firms that specialise in boat trailing if the owner thinks his boat may be too much for his own car. During the season, however, they will need a permanent mooring or reserved berth in a marina, where they can be left safely when not in use. In choosing this permanent base you will therefore need to consider how often you hope to use the boat and the length of journey to and from home, even if this inescapably points you to an area that would not otherwise be your first choice. You will probably need to make a reconnaissance to look at possibilities, talk to boatyards and find out what is available and at what price. Don't forget to find out about winter lay-up, if you are not bringing the boat home, or about the launching possibilities if you trail, but you have to be prepared to be allocated an outside mooring berth, probably far from the landing hard, as the demand is now so great that you will be lucky to find the ideal one straight away. Do start looking about for a mooring even before you begin negotiating for your boat. There can be nothing more infuriating than having a beautiful boat (even if it is second-hand) and finding there is nowhere to berth it. Remember, anchoring, which we shall come to later, is not desirable for a boat that is to be left for more than a few hours.

Obtaining up-to-date information
We should like to give you a quick guide to the British

coast, telling you what facilities to expect in each main area. Unfortunately the yachting scene changes so fast nowadays that this would be out of date even before this book was printed. For the same reason you need to look at the date of any pilot book you are using, as most are not reprinted annually and may be partly out of date before the next edition appears. There is a marina book that does issue annual additions, but most pilot books don't.

As a very broad guide, it is worth saying that in the Solent area you can expect to find little other than marinas or trots. From there marinas have been spreading east and west, reaching to Devon in one direction and into Suffolk in the other, but beyond this vague generalisation you just have to make enquiries.

There is no organisation in cruising similar to the National Caravan Council, producing an annual index of sites. The Royal Yachting Association is concerned mainly with more general matters of policy, not with detail. Of the other clubs and associations, the one with far the best detailed, up-to-date information is the Cruising Association. This publishes a handbook covering the whole of the British Isles and neighbouring foreign coasts. It is not and cannot be an annual publication because it is far too expensive to produce, containing as it does harbour plans and navigational instructions and details of anchorages, moorings and yacht harbours as well as other facilities. What is even more important is that this information is kept up to date in a thoroughly practical way — by individual members sending in information obtained on their own cruises. Those who have bought the handbook, which is available to non-members for £8 can also, for a small sum, get the annual list of changes, while for members, notes of the main changes are sent out three times a year with the Association's Bulletin.

Membership of the Association is not cheap — £12 a year with a £5 entrance fee and a special subscription of only £3 for wives, but the facilities offered are considerable: a cruise planning section containing a comprehensive collection of charts, supplemented by members' notes on different areas, which are often too full to publish, one of the largest nautical libraries in the country in the headquarters in St Katharine's Dock near Tower Bridge and a full programme of winter talks and courses in London, with rapidly growing programmes in many regional centres, to mention only a few. It is an association where you can meet and talk to others who enjoy cruising and which produces an annual owners and crew list, to help those who need boats and those who need crews to get together. Ownership of a boat is not compulsory for membership and someone keen to learn could do worse than consider joining.

Part 3

A First Cruise in Tidal Waters

The first venture into tidal waters is perhaps the most critical period in anyone's cruising career. If it's a success you will be bitten for life; if it's a failure you may never cruise again. It is so different from inland waterways that enjoyment of one does not necessarily mean equal enjoyment of the other. It is never easy to predict how anyone will react to a new and strange way of life, particularly if this is a family venture and each individual is likely to react differently. What makes this first cruise extra hazardous is that it has to fulfil a dual purpose — you will at the same time be educating yourselves nautically and learning to live afloat.

And so in this section we are going to try to convey to you the feeling of being afloat by taking you on a typical cruise with an average family on its first venture. We will call them the Smiths — Paul and Jean the parents, with their children, Mark aged twelve and Diana ten. We will assume that they went up the Thames together the previous year and since then Paul, who had sailed with friends before his marriage, has brushed up his rusty knowledge by reading and a weekend at a sailing school. Anyhow, he has enough experience to satisfy the Charter Company that he can be trusted with a yacht in coastal waters, and he has assured them that he won't go far. He is perhaps relieved that he need not admit that none of his crew have ever sailed and that his attempts to instil a little elementary knowledge during the winter weren't quite as successful as he had hoped. Somehow or other the sessions were always cut short because Jean wanted to cook or Mark showed unusual enthusiasm for his homework or Diana started to fidget and upset everybody else.

They have decided that the Harwich estuary is the place for them and are starting from Pin Mill on the river Orwell. They have been told to be there by 11.30 a.m. — otherwise they will not be able to get afloat until the afternoon tide brings water back to the hard. Paul isn't very popular when he tells them to be ready by eight o'clock. The family is not good at getting up, even with the excitement of a holiday and he can hear the children muttering about fussy old dad who always gets them there hours too soon. In fact they don't start at eight — they are an hour late and with one or two hold-ups on the road it is after midday before they reach Pin Mill. The water already looks a long way away; small boats are lying about on the mud at all sorts of unusual angles and there seems to be little activity as they walk down the hard — a sort of flight path built up over mud to facilitate

44

getting ashore. When they reach the end there is indeed a gap between them and the water, made up of very soft, deep squelchy mud. The children are learning, the hard way, their first lesson on:

The importance of tides

For the next fortnight the Smiths are to become increasingly conscious of the fact that life is dominated by tide time rather than clock time. There are places like Pin Mill where it is not possible to get ashore at low tide — or of course to get back to the boat from the shore. As we have already seen, there are marinas and inner basins of harbours where entry is possible only at certain states of the tide; access may be limited to as little as one hour in twelve, near high water. If you have to wait for the tide to get into a marina it may be a nuisance. Worse still, you may have to wait to get into some rivers such as the Deben and the Alde on the East Coast, which have a shallow bar at the entrance giving only a foot or two of water at low tide. How long you will have to wait if you arrive at the wrong moment will depend on the draught of your boat, but it can often be uncomfortable hanging around out at sea and may give you some anxious moments if the wind is rising or the visibility deteriorating. The upper reaches of many rivers and creeks can be explored only when the tide is high and you may get yourself shut in for a few hours by forgetting that there is a shallow patch — a 'horse' it is usually called — below you, which prevents you from getting down river, even though you have plenty of water to lie afloat where you have anchored.

It is not only the depth of water that you have to consider. The tides will also affect the time you take on any passage. Your own speed may be no more than a fast walking pace — say 4 knots. If you have a tide against you of 1½ knots your actual speed *over the ground* will be reduced to 2½ knots. Conversely, of course, if the tide is with you, you will make not 4 but 5½ knots over the ground. It does not need much calculation to see how much difference it will make, even on a short passage, if you manage to use the tides and you soon learn that if the tide tells you to go at 4 a.m. you go. Most of us dislike struggling out of bed at these inhuman hours, but it is surprising how often one is rewarded by a lovely morning, with all the opalescent colours of the pre-dawn sky culminating in a glorious sunrise.

Getting aboard — the dinghy

Now to return to our family. It is a rather deflated party that walks back up the hard and sits at the edge to eat the picnic lunch they had hoped to enjoy aboard. The tide seems to take hours to turn, (indeed it can be up to an hour each side of the tide tables) and it is after two o'clock before all the boats out on the moorings have turned to face downstream, pointing into the incoming tide. The representative of the charter firm has found them by now and arranged that he will take Jean, Diana and their gear over in the yard boat while Paul rows Mark over in the dinghy. There are protests from Mark, who is rather proud of his swimming, when he is made to put on a life jacket and even Jean wonders if her husband isn't being a bit fussy on a calm day, but he remains adamant. There are more accidents he has read, going to and from the yacht by dinghy than when aboard and he thinks it safer for the children to wear life jackets automatically in the dinghy — apart from anything else it will save argument if it becomes routine — and he and Jean intend to follow suit if it is at all rough.

Still rather disgruntled, Mark tries to jump into the dinghy and lands in a heap in the bottom. His father roars with laughter.

'Good thing it's an inflatable,' he says. 'You'd have been testing that life jacket with any other sort of dinghy.'

He goes on to explain how important it is to move gently and keep your balance whether getting in or out of dinghies, even with an inflatable, which is far more difficult to upset than other types.

The choice of dinghy is one of the most perplexing problems with which a yachtsman is confronted, because you are always asking for the impossible. You want something small enough to stow on deck to avoid having to tow it on long sea passages, yet large enough to take the whole crew and still have a reasonable amount of freeboard. You need something light enough to carry up a hard, but stable enough to be safe in moderately rough water, a dinghy which rows well, tows well and will remain balanced, whether you have any number aboard from one to four or five and whether you are rowing or using an outboard motor. No one has yet found the ideal answer and the final decision is a compromise and a matter of individual judgment. Some will go for a small light dinghy knowing that two or three journeys will be needed to get all the crew onshore; others will choose something larger which may be a nuisance in other ways, particularly on a wild night at moorings. Whichever you choose you should never overload it, for that is asking for an accident.

If however, you are planning anything except short sea passages, in a smallish yacht of say 32 feet or less you really have no choice. You *must* be able to get the dinghy aboard under conditions when it is too rough to tow it safely, and no hard dinghy suitable for a crew of four or five will be stowable on deck and still leave you room to work the sails. In a motor boat, where the deck isn't essential working space, it is much easier. All you can do therefore in a small yacht is to use an inflatable, which you bring aboard half deflated. In an emergency you can throw it overboard and it will remain afloat while you blow up the other half, thus acting as a life raft, for which you may have no room, as well as a dinghy. And for this reason you *must* have a hand pump and not a foot pump, which you cannot operate when in the water.

From all other points of view, the inflatable has nothing to commend it. It is no fun to row at any time and impossible against a strong wind, so under some conditions it is useless without an outboard motor and some of these, as you will discover, have their foibles.

By this time the family is aboard and on its own after checking the inventory and being shown the layout of the rigging and how to work the engine and the sea toilet. There is a gentle rocking, with the occasional violent lurch as someone moves clumsily and Jean, surrounded by kitbags and boxes, is looking a bit unhappy. The children are getting restless and clamouring for their first sail. Their hopes are raised when Paul shows them how to make sail. But one glance down below when this is finished is enough to show that Jean isn't nearly ready and that there is only one thing Paul can do to help — keep the children out of the way. Fortunately they leap at his suggestion that they should go and test the dinghy outboard and perhaps try their hand at rowing as well.

Left to herself, Jean gets on faster and is sitting in the cockpit looking rather thoughtful by the time they return. It is all rather different from anything she had imagined and she had somehow never grasped the implication of lying on a swinging mooring, that they could not get ashore without going in that beastly little rubber thing, which she was sure none of them would be able to manage. She couldn't help remembering those days on the Thames the previous year when the atmosphere had got a bit tense as one or other of the family got itchy feet or short-tempered. After a day or two she had been able to spot the signs in advance and avert trouble by suggesting that they pulled into the bank for half an hour to go for a walk. This time it didn't look as if there would be any bank to pull into, however restive or quarrelsome the children; they would have to learn how to live with each other cooped up in a little box. She wondered, indeed, whether she might not get claustrophobia herself at times. She was used to an active life.

Diana's shrill voice as the dinghy returned must have been heard right down the river. Mark is rowing and his father instructing him in coming alongside. There is a giggle from Diana as he misses and shoots past under the stern, but next time he does better and soon they are all back aboard chattering excitedly. They are told firmly to

49

stop talking and concentrate while Mark is left to see that the dinghy is tied on firmly. Jean looks surprised — at home Mark isn't generally regarded as a reliable type!

Shipping forecasts

At ten to six Paul turns on the radio, tuning in to Radio 2. At 5.55 p.m. they hear the words, which were soon to become familiar: 'Here is the Shipping Forecast issued by the Meteorological Office at … '

Bad weather can spoil any holiday, but on a boat it is going to affect your lives in ways that don't concern you on dry land. It doesn't matter whether it is going to be hot or cold; it doesn't even matter all that much whether it's going to be wet or dry, except that wet weather tends to be accompanied by bad visibility. What does matter is what the wind is likely to do, and when the forecast starts off, 'There are warnings of gales in … ' you listen anxiously to see whether your area is likely to be affected. Wind strength and direction may determine where you go next day and will also suggest, unless you are in a marina, where you should go to get a peaceful night. We shall come back to this when we talk about anchoring, but first a word about the forecasts themselves.

Broadcast four times a day — at 0033, 0633, 1355 (1155 on Sundays) and 1755 — on BBC Radio 2, Long Wave, 1500 metres, these forecasts, which are intended for *all* shipping, cover an area from about mid-Atlantic to Sweden and from Iceland to Spain. This is sub-divided into 29 forecast areas of varying size and each with a distinctive name. Humber, Thames, Dover, Wight, Portland, Plymouth are a few of the more obvious round the East and South coasts of England. Each of these areas except Humber extends right across the North Sea or Channel to the coasts of Holland, Belgium or France, so it is obvious that there is not always uniformity of weather over the whole area. Winds, for example are often less strong up the coast than in the middle of the North Sea. A chart of these forecast areas is given in Reed's and any book on meteorology and special pads for taking down the forecasts can be obtained from yacht chandlers for anyone who wants to take forecasting seriously.

After any gale warnings the forecasts start with a general synopsis giving the main pattern of depressions, fronts and high pressure areas with their anticipated movements. It is not unlike a more detailed version of a normal television forecast and by now most of us are so accustomed to looking at weather maps that it is not difficult to visualise what is happening. After this, there is a detailed forecast for each area giving wind force and direction and likely changes in both, weather conditions and visibility. Finally there are reports of what was happening two or three hours before at thirteen weather stations either on the coast or on weather ships.

The strength of the wind is indicated by numbers on what is known as the Beaufort scale, ranging from 1–12. Force 0 is calm, Force 5 a fresh breeze (17–21 knots) and Force 8 gale (34–40 knots). It is unusual in British waters to find a wind stronger than Force 10, Storm (48–55 knots). The ideal strength for a day's sea sailing is about Force 4.

There are two things to concentrate on when listening to these forecasts: the current picture in your area and possible future movements. If for example you are in area

Thames, which has a good forecast, and the forecast for Plymouth predicts a deep depression moving east with gale force winds, you can anticipate that the gale may reach you within the next day or so and that if you want to make a coastal passage you had better take your chance today before it arrives. As we all know, the forecasters are not always right. They are the first to admit that they are occasionally fooled by depressions, the speed with which they will move and whether they will deepen or fill, but if you listen to shipping forecasts regularly you will be surprised how often they are right, and if the future forecast is bad it is as well, at sea, to assume the worst.

From the moment you get aboard, therefore, you should get into the habit of listening to at least one shipping forecast a day. It's no good thinking that because you are going to stay in the river for the next three days it doesn't matter. You will have lost track of the general picture and probably find that when you do want to make a passage the weather is impossible. For most of us, I suspect, it is the forecast at 1755 hours which is heard most frequently, because by that time one has snugged down for the night and it is just the right time for the evening drink in the cockpit when the forecast is over. But, if there are gales around we try to listen to at least one other in the 24 hours; after a few days aboard we tend to wake automatically about half past six in time for the early morning forecast. If you are planning a long sea passage you should also hear the forecast nearest to your time of departure, though this tends to be a counsel of perfection if there is to be a near dawn start. Everybody likes to go to bed early and the thought of spoiling a short night by waking up for the forecast at 0033 is not attractive.

The main shipping forecasts are supplemented by Inshore Waters Forecast on Radio 4 at midnight. Less detailed than the main shipping forecasts, it is nevertheless a useful adjunct and for coastal cruising may be more accurate than forecasts for a wider area.

Picking up moorings

The forecast over, Paul suggests it is time for an evening drink and puts out a bottle of sherry, two glasses and two tins of 'coke'. The family gather in the cockpit, where Paul has a quick glance at Mark's knot — a bit un-nautical, he thinks, but at least the dinghy will not float away. As they drink a toast to a happy holiday, everyone seems to have accepted without further discussion the fact that it is now too late to start sailing that evening. Several yachts come up river, with crews getting active on the foredeck as they prepare to drop sails before picking up their moorings.

It can, of course, be done under sail, but nowadays moorings are so congested that there isn't much room; if you make a mistake, or there's a bad gust of wind at the wrong moment, you may damage someone else's boat as well as your own, so unless you really are a skilled helmsman it is safer to use the auxiliary engine when picking up or leaving moorings.

They watch, fascinated, as some boats come in with the sails neatly furled and make a good job of mooring, while others look untidy and have to dab at the moorings two or three times before catching the buoy. Mark shouts gleefully when a rather distraught looking woman misses completely. His unflattering remarks to his sister about women are interrupted by a reminder to keep his voice down because voices carry so far across the water, and a promise that they will all have a good laugh the first time he misses his pick-up. Often, Paul explains, the poor old foredeck hand is blamed when it is the helmsman who has made a mess of it by misjudging the distance or going too fast.

The visiting yacht in a strange harbour or river

The last yacht to come in is circling round, uncertain where to go and finally one of the crew asks Paul if he knows whether the next-door mooring is free for the night. Paul has to admit he is a stranger too and the new yacht finally picks up and starts to bag the sails. This is quite a normal occurrence, because once you are on a cruise you will naturally be away from your own base and looking for a mooring or berth in someone else's anchorage, while leaving your own vacant. It suits everybody therefore that there should be a free and informal interchange of moorings and in general this works very well provided everybody observes certain common courtesies. The procedure is:

1. If there is a harbour master or boatman to be seen make contact and ask him to allocate you a mooring. Before doing so he may ask your weight and draught; you on your side should offer him his fees immediately.
2. If there is nobody about, pick up any *suitable*

mooring until you can discover whether it is free. By suitable we mean one which is strong enough for your boat, as all moorings are not of the same weight; they are laid to suit the boat that normally uses them. Occasionally you will find the maximum weight marked on the buoy, but more often you will have to judge for yourself. If the chain is much lighter than that to which you are accustomed, or if all the other boats in that line of moorings are smaller than yours, the mooring is probably too light and you should look for another or go and anchor. A boat that drags its mooring on a wild night can do untold damage as it bumps its way down river, savaging other boats as it goes.

A dinghy left on a mooring is usually a sign that the owner intends to return shortly. The mooring should not be picked up.

3. If you are going ashore you must go at once to find the boatman to ask whether you may stay on the mooring. Remember to look at the number or name on the mooring, or note the name of the neighbouring boats, so that you can tell him where you are. Ideally you should leave sufficient crew aboard to move the boat if the owner comes back, but if this is impractable, as it often is with a family crew, at least you should stay within sight of the mooring until you have discovered whether it is free.

4. If you are not going ashore you can just stay and wait for the boatman to find you or the owner to return, provided you don't make a fuss if the latter happens in the middle of the night!

5. Under all circumstances and even if you have paid

the dues for the mooring you MUST move at once, and graciously, if the owner returns. You are there as a matter of courtesy and not by right.

In a strange marina, the procedure is much the same. There may be a notice at the entrance directing you to the visitors' pontoon or you may see the boatman indicating a berth. If not, go into any empty berth and tie up temporarily while you go off to find the Harbour Master to ask where he would like you to go. Even in a visitors' berth, it is as well to report your arrival as soon as you have tied up and pay your dues.

A first sail

It is an excited little family next morning that prepares for the first day's sail, so excited indeed that everything takes twice as long as usual. For Paul it is one of the most frustrating mornings he has ever spent. He is so eager for the family to enjoy sailing and the wind is perfect for a first effort, but here they are forgetting everything he has shown them the previous afternoon. Diana proudly shows Jean how to set the foresail — but gets it upside down, while Mark, left to sort out sheets and halyards, produces a wonderful tangle. Jean who has missed the previous day's explanations looks a bit bewildered. Several times Paul is tempted to go and do everything himself just to get under way, but at last, as far as he can see, the sails and rigging are ready for hoisting. He hasn't fallen into the trap of giving up trying to get the family to start doing things. If he had done everything himself in desperation they would have learnt nothing.

Somewhat nervously Paul starts the motor, shouts to

Mark to drop the mooring overboard and they are off! They had all agreed that they'd better get round the corner before making (hoisting) sail so that, if there was a shambles, as Mark put it, at least they would be out of sight of the pub and everyone on the hard. As it turns out, it all goes rather well and the only help Paul has to give is to go on deck and *swig* (tighten) up the sails. He makes a mental note that he would like mast winches on his own boat to help. Then comes the blissful silence as the engine is turned off and the boat comes alive as it starts to move through the water under sail. Some of the family gasp as it heels a little, but Paul explains that this is normal in a sailing boat. It can be alarming for the beginner, particularly when a sudden gust catches the sail and the boat heels even further than you expect, but in normal circumstances there is no danger. It does mean, however, that any jobs you need to do aboard are difficult when under way. Just moving about the cabin is an effort, while you cannot open any cupboard on the windward (high) side without the contents cascading out — you soon learn!

Anchoring

The technique of anchoring
By the time everyone has had a turn at the helm and they have been across Harwich harbour and back Jean is complaining that her hands are sore with sheeting in, while Mark and Diana are clamouring for food. They go back a little way up river past Shotley spit where Paul proposes to anchor for lunch. As they approach the spot he tells them to take the sails down and tie them up. With

the motor running slowly he edges in until the echo sounder shows twelve feet, then he shouts to Jean to drop the anchor. She is surprised to find how easily she manages to do it. There is nothing in anchor work that most women cannot manage, but one or two tips (which do not appear in most books written by, and apparently exclusively for, men) may be helpful. First, always keep your hands well away from the chain roller. Secondly, do not hang on like grim death if the chain which you are trying to pay out runs away with you. This will only occur occasionally when anchoring against a very fast tide, but if you try to hang on, it will pull you forward into the roller, risking the loss of quite a lot of skin if not of a finger or two. The only course is to drop the chain and then jump on it to prevent it coming up with a jerk which might damage the boat. Thirdly, when getting the anchor in, don't strain. It will come up quite easily if it is straight up and down, but when it lies taut out ahead you are trying to pull the weight of the boat, while if it is at right angles to or underneath the boat it jams. So, if the anchor is in the wrong position just take a turn of the chain round the samson post and wait until the boat either swings or is manoeuvred back into the right position. Then pull in a little more until it gets difficult again, when you take another turn round the post. In this way you are making the boat do most of the work for you.

Choosing an anchorage
Theoretically you can anchor anywhere (except in the middle of mooring where there will not be room for you to swing and your anchor will probably catch in a

Kala Sona in distinguished company at St. Katharine's Dock, Tower Bridge. Each year that goes by you will be more likely to find yourself spending the night on this sort of 'finger' marina staging, whether abroad or along the coasts of Britain.

mooring chain and be impossible to pull up) so long as you are out of the way of other boats. Particularly avoid a buoyed channel for commercial vessels.

In practice, however, it is not as simple as that. For a start, you need to find a spot where your type of anchor will hold and this depends on the nature of the river bed. In hard clay or kelp, a plough (CQR) anchor may not even dig in and you need a fisherman type; in shingle it may find nothing to grip; among rocks it may grip only too well and jam so hard that you cannot get it up again; in kelp it may catch on the seaweed and never reach the bottom — it will hold for a time and then start to drag —

Waldringfield moorings (River Deben). On the East Coast we are still lucky enough to swing from individual moorings in the shadow of hospitable inns like the Maybush from which this shot was taken.

probably at four o'clock in the morning. Secondly, if you want to anchor in the shelter of a bank, choose one which is reasonably steep to. On a very shallow, gently shelving shore you may be near the middle of the river before you can find enough depth to stay afloat at low water. So you lose any shelter you may get from the bank, apart from the possibility of obstructing other traffic.

Finally, choose an anchorage if possible where there is reasonable shelter from the wind direction prevailing that day. A long straight reach is hopeless unless the wind is off-shore and you can tuck in under the bank on the weather side. Each little bay will provide shelter in some winds and be untenable in others. What you have to remember is that it is surprising how rough it can be, even in a river, if you are at the end of a reach where the waves can build up, and there is nothing that makes many of us seasick so quickly as rolling about at anchor.

In most rivers there are enough twists and turns to provide a sheltered spot somewhere, whatever the wind. Just crossing to the other bank could make all the difference, but this is one reason why it is so important to listen to the shipping forecast before settling down for the night. The pilot books will probably mark the most likely spots — particularly those where landing is possible — it is up to you to choose the best one for any particular day.

One last point, if other boats are already anchored, be sure to give them plenty of room, always remembering you will all swing at change of tide. If you anchor too close and give the next boat a 'foul berth' it is your fault — and it will be you, or your Insurance Company, that pays for any damage to other boats. Anchoring for the night you are expected to show a riding light — an all-round white light at the forward end of the boat.

Exploring the 'Secret waters'

For three days the novelty of the life, combined with the challenge of learning something of the varied jobs which make up crewing on a small yacht, would be enough to keep the family happy as they sail up and down the Orwell, the Stour and several times across Harwich Harbour. They anchor each day for lunch as well as for the night and Paul takes care to see that at one anchorage they can get ashore. It is a good excuse for dinghy practice and he suspects that they aren't ready yet for a whole day without stretching their legs. He has had to be firm with Jean once or twice when she tries to revert to her normal role as wife and mother, leaving all the nautical activity and all the fun to the children. He has had to be equally firm with the children that they are to do their share of the domestic chores. It's all part of being a crew, he tells them, and there is an unwritten rule on boats that the cook never does the washing up.

The third afternoon Diana complains that the water pump is not working. She is soon disillusioned and told that they have all been too extravagant with water. On the Thames the problem had never arisen as they had filled up each day, but here it is different. Filling up means going ashore in the dinghy with two cans and bringing them back and tipping them into the tank. Now the tank was empty it would take four journeys — not a bright prospect with a family not yet strong enough to carry the heavy cans, and Paul emphasises he isn't going to do this every other day. This time, in fact they are lucky. They can just slip across the Orwell to Levington Marina where there will be piped water on the pontoons and they can fill up by hose.

It was in Levington that Paul decided they were due for a change of scene and to Diana's excitement suggested that they might go across to Arthur Ransome's 'Secret Waters', the Walton Backwaters. She had been enchanted by the book but hadn't believed that they really existed. There is something near peace for half an hour as Paul tells them to sit down with *East Coast Rivers* and learn all the buoys that mark the channel into the Backwaters so that they can spot them the next day and there isn't a word of complaint when he also tells them that, to catch the tide, they will be starting at eight o'clock the next morning.

The next few days are enchanting. For part of each day they anchor off Stone Point, where there is a steep sandy beach and they can go ashore and enjoy a swim. When Jean has to be taken down to Walton to shop, the children choose to stay on Sandy Point and play desert islands.

Going aground

Part of each day is spent in sailing practice, and Paul watches their progress with interest. To his surprise the one who shows the most flair is Diana. Despite the difficulty that she is a little short to see over the cabin top, she is the only one who really seems to feel the boat and treat it as if it is something alive, like a horse. Jean is becoming very safe and sound and Mark very confident, and inclined to show off by sailing very fast and very far heeled over, partly because he knows his sister dislikes it. It is in one of these moods that he leaves his tack too late and goes aground. His father, who was in the cabin, feels the boat stop and hears the sails flapping.

He is up the steps into the cockpit in no time, telling Mark to get the sails down and Jean to get the dinghy alongside. The family is so shaken by the peremptory tone that they respond with unusual speed. It is only a couple of minutes before Paul is rowing the anchor out in the dinghy and dropping it in deeper water. Before he gets back aboard he shouts to them to pull and get over onto the port side to heel the boat. At first nothing

" ... It would have been ten or eleven hours before they floated again and in the meantime they would have looked 'right Charlies'!"

happens, then slowly the boat slithers through the mud. As soon as she moves, Paul is back aboard and has the engine started to motor them out into mid stream. In any case it is nearly time for them to find an anchorage for the night and there is unspoken agreement that sailing practice has finished for the day. Mark is rather quiet and unusually thorough as he busies himself tidying up the sails and it is not until they have anchored and are resting that he asks the question which is in all their minds: what would have happened if they hadn't been able to pull themselves off?

Nothing, he is told except an uncomfortable night. It was only one hour after high tide when they went aground, so it would have been ten or eleven hours before they floated again and in the meantime they would have looked 'right Charlies'! The dinghy would have been aground too, so they would not even have been able to go for a row. In the soft mud of the Walton Backwaters it would be difficult to come to any harm, but on the sand banks out at sea it would have been a different matter. 'Those are as hard as granite and if it's rough when the tide comes in you may bump on them so hard before you float, that you knock your bottom out', Paul tells them.

Anchored in the creeks
Much as they enjoyed the rest of the day, the anchorages in the evening were really the best of all. Then they were in quiet creeks, at times hemmed in between precipitous little mud banks, at others looking out over half-submerged marshes where the reeds seemed to grow out of the water. Rather like a lift going up and down they thought, even if it did take six hours. They explored the smaller creeks by dinghy, an ideal place for them all to get used to dinghy work. Jean started to sketch — she hadn't done anything for years — while Diana discovered what a wonderful place a boat was for her latest hobby, bird watching. At low water all the waders came down on the mud to feed and potter about within a few yards of the boat, taking no notice of it so long as there is no sudden movement. Fish played about round the dinghy, but they had no fishing gear aboard, and anyhow, Jean said, they probably wouldn't have caught anything.

A mini-cruise up the coast

It was such an idyllic life that it was tempting just to stay

65

in the Backwaters for the rest of their holiday, but Paul thought that this might give them too rosy an idea of cruising and that it was time to take them for a short sea passage, to the Deben, four miles up the coast. Reluctantly they are dragged in from their other amusements to try on their safety harnesses and make sure they understand where to clip themselves on in case they have to do anything on deck. They are not, Paul insisted, to go on deck without them and if it is at all rough they will be wearing life jackets too. They discuss whether to take seasick pills and decide to risk it, and finally, half deflated, the dinghy is put on deck.

After all the preparations, the passage itself was almost an anti-climax. It was dead calm and there wasn't a breath of wind. Much as the children were longing to sail, they were told firmly that it was pointless even to hang the sails up and that in any case there was no time for messing about. The Deben is one of the rivers with a nasty bar, which restricts entry to about three hours or less either side of high water, and on the ebb the water pours out of the narrow entrance at about $5\frac{1}{2}$ knots, which was faster than they could motor. So they had to get there before high tide or wait another nine hours, and by then it would be dark.

With nothing to do, Mark and Diana quickly get bored. At first they are happily occupied spotting all the buoys in the big ship channel and Paul tries to fill in the time by showing them how to pinpoint their position by taking bearings, but Diana does not really get the hang of it and begins to look a little green when they go down below to try to plot the position on the chart. For all the calm conditions there is an unpleasant roll and Diana is not the only one who is relieved when the Deben buoy is sighted and they are told they will soon be in the river.

Sea sickness

Most beginners, especially children, are rather ashamed of themselves if they are seasick. They needn't be, because the doctors estimate that it is only about five per cent of the population who are immune from the trouble, while at the other end of the scale there is another ten per cent who would feel ill on any boat in the calmest of sheltered waters. For the rest of us, therefore, who feel ill in varying degrees, it is a question of learning to cope. Most of us are worse at the beginning of a passage than when we have been aboard a few days. Many are all right if they are either out in the fresh air or lying down in the cabin. It is doing things down below which is trying and one of the most dangerous periods is the few minutes it takes to struggle into your oilskins and get on deck after you have been off watch. Some find that as long as they are sick they can recover at once; others just have to go and lie down. If you are not too bad, a few deep breaths can avert an attack.

But for most of us nowadays there is some hope in modern pills, which are very effective. The only trouble is that there are different sorts and it seems a matter of chance which type suits any individual. You may have an uncomfortable passage or two before your experiments show which is the type for you, but once you have discovered this you can probably ensure that you rarely suffer from seasickness, provided that you take the pills in good time. It is useless waiting until you feel ill — then they'll only make you worse.

An exchange of visits

On this passage we will assume that the light is good and spotting the meets — the leading marks which direct you through this tricky entrance — is easier than it can be in bad visibility. The wind is getting up by now so they make sail in the river and breathe with relief as the engine is turned off. They soon decide they do not want to stay at Felixstowe Ferry near the mouth, but will push on to

Ramsholt on the Deben

Ramsholt further up, with its old barge quay and pub. At Ramsholt they decide to go a little further on and look at an anchorage known as the Rocks where there is another of the sandy beaches so rare along this part of the coast. One glance tells them that this is the place. There is only one other boat anchored and Mark and Diana are by now impatient to get ashore. It actually takes them a little longer than they expected because they have forgotten that they will have to blow up the dinghy first, but soon they are all ashore, the children swim while their parents go for a walk.

By the time they return they find that the young have made friends with the teenagers from the other boat and inform them casually that they have been invited back aboard for coffee. At first you may feel hesitant about accepting this sort of invitation, but you will soon discover how friendly most people are when cruising and an exchange of visits is all part of the fun. Most boat owners are both inordinately proud of their own boat, eager to show it off, and insatiably curious about other boats they get a chance to visit. For the beginner, such visits are a real godsend because the more you can see of different types of boats, the better equipped you will be when it comes to choosing your own. Never feel that you will be thought inquisitive if you ask to go below and look around; apart from ideas on layout you'll pick up all sorts of useful ideas on fittings and gadgets. As we shall discover when we get to Part 4, ingenuity in making the best use of a restricted space is an essential quality and most people love to show you their inventions.

Before going back to their own boat Mark announces firmly that he had made plans for the next day. His new friend has a sailing dinghy and has promised to take them out in it. When Jean looks doubtful, Paul jumps at the chance for his son to get some useful sailing practice and agrees that they will go up river to Waldringfield to shop and leave the children to their own devices.

Young children aboard

When they get back from shopping next day Paul and Jean discover that another boat has arrived and that all the families are ashore enjoying a picnic. They go over to join them. The newcomers have two very young children with them, aged only two and three. They run about in their life jackets, which they wear all the time so that it's as natural to put them on as the rest of their clothes. They look enchanting, but Jean asks how they manage at that age.

Small babies aboard at the carry-cot stages are no problem provided you have space for all the special gear and food that you need. Toddlers, however, are more of a problem. It is not just a question of ensuring that an active child does not fall in — safety can be guaranteed by using life jackets and harnessess during the day, car seats can be used at meal times while canvas sides can be attached to the bunks to prevent them from falling out at night. But you will have to gear your programme to the fact that any normal cruise is just not on with young children aboard. For a start, you will lose the services of your wife as an active member of crew — she will be too busy keeping the children happy — and you will not be able to make more than the occasional sea passage. You can get away with some passages by sailing by night, but by day it is generally reckoned that one passage every four days is the most you can manage; to keep the children happy you will have to allow them the other three days to enjoy themselves playing on the sand.

A wet day
It is a beautiful evening and the party ashore forgets about the shipping forecast for once. Nobody notices the mares' tail clouds which are beginning to streak the sky. It's quite a surprise to be woken up about two o'clock by the gentle patter of rain on the cabin roof. The wind is beginning to rise also and as the boat rocks uneasily the

slap of waves on her sides becomes more insistent and there is a rat-tat-tat as the halyards are rattled against the mast. I must make a better job of frapping (securing the halyards) tomorrow, Paul thinks, as he goes back to sleep.

By the morning it is really pouring and blowing half a gale. Paul can see through the portholes that the other boats are sheering about and sailing round their anchors, but at least they all seem to be in the same relative positions, so presumably nobody's anchor has dragged. The children are a bit gloomy at breakfast and ask what they are going to do. They become even gloomier when Paul tells them that it is too rough for them to go off in the dinghy and that, as he isn't going to dress up in full oilskins to take them calling, they will just have to amuse themselves aboard. There is an imminent argument because Mark has finished all the available books, except that which Diana is reading and she refuses to part with it. Paul averts trouble for the moment by suggesting that he would like help with a little engine maintenance, as he isn't too happy with the way it is running and would prefer to check it over at anchor and avoid the possibility of working on it out at sea. Even this does not at first arouse much enthusiasm, until he explains how essential it is to be able to do everything yourself if you want to own a boat and you really need an assistant mechanic aboard, as this seems the one job the women are not too good at. Finally Paul manages to get his son interested and there is peace for a time as they work together, while the others curl up on the bunks with their books.

This gets them through the morning and it is not until after lunch that the next crisis looms up. 'What are we going to play?' the young ask — 'Why couldn't we have brought Monopoly?' Jean tries to explain gently that it takes up rather a lot of room and she didn't know whether there would be stowage space for it. She suggests bridge, which they are just starting to learn, but for the moment they are too disgruntled at being deprived of their favourite game to concentrate and they finally settle down to rummy or vingt-et-un. It is still pouring as if it would never stop, but after dinner they are lucky and it eases off, so, with relief, they bale out the dinghy and go ashore for a walk.

Whether your crew consists of family or friends, a few really bad days provide one of the biggest tests to which they can be subjected. It isn't so bad in a yacht harbour, where anyone who gets desperate can dress up in full oilies and go for a walk, but on a mooring or at anchor one is more reluctant to dress up to go ashore by dinghy and if the wind is strong it may be impossible to do so safely. The worst we have experienced was a whole week when the wind was never less than gale force 8 and on only two days could we get off the boat. Fortunately the friends who were with us that week were as happy as we were to spend most of the time playing bridge, but it doesn't take much imagination to see how quickly friction can build up in these circumstances. Silly little habits can become irritating; for some, lack of exercise is a worry, while sheer boredom can destroy the morale of any crew. Few people who lead a normally active life are happy to sit and read *all* day long, so the boat's equipment must include some game or occupation in which everyone can join, but even with this the skipper or mate needs to be alert for signs of tension and exercise a little of what the Services used to call 'Man-Management' before it is too late.

An uncomfortable sea passage
Three days later the Smiths find that the weather still hasn't settled down and the forecast promises a SW wind force 5 — a head wind for return to Harwich and a bit on the strong side too. Time is now running short; only two days remain before the boat has to be back in Pin Mill and it is never advisable to leave even a short sea passage to the last possible moment. If the day after were to bring a south-westerly gale it might be impossible to return.

In these conditions, maximum safety precautions must be taken and everybody dressed up in oilskins and life jackets as well as in safety harnesses. There may be some moaning about feeling like a Christmas tree and being unable to move, but the odd mutterings about 'silly old Dad' will soon stop when they discover a horrible, lumpy sea outside the river and when another boat comes past, crewed by lusty young men all similarly togged up the children will begin to feel rather pleased with themselves and very nautical. This is just as well because the wind, instead of diminishing as forecast, is obviously increasing and soon they discover that, even though they had already reefed down, they were still over-canvassed for the conditions. It is all a bit worrying because two of them will have to go on deck, first to change to a smaller headsail and also to roll a bit more of the mainsail round the boom — Paul would be thankful that the boat at least has roller reefing which can be done from the mast and doesn't necessitate crew working too far from a strong hitch-on point.

The question now, however, is who shall go forward? It is not going to be easy working up there on a deck which is pitching fairly violently; on the other hand it is going to take some skill at the helm to keep to wind while the sail changing is going on. Paul explains the difficulty to Jean. Neither child, they agreed, should be left with the responsibility at the tiller and Diana was too young for the deck work either under these conditions. Before Paul could get any further, he was surprised to find Jean telling him that it was she and Mark who would be changing the sails, because at no price would she be left in charge of the tiller. The wind was getting worse and there was no time for argument so reluctantly Paul agreed. The job seemed interminable and Mark looked as relieved as Paul when he got back into the cockpit. He glanced anxiously at Jean as she followed. To his surprise she looked as if she had positively enjoyed herself.

Soon after this they started to get a bit of shelter from the land and with a day still in hand decided to return to their favourite anchorage in Landermere Creek for the night.

Plans for the future

It is surprising how quickly one recovers from a bad passage. The sense of achievement — and there are few yachtsmen so blasé that they don't feel this even after years of experience — mingled with relief that it is all over, brings a wonderful sense of well-being and here in a quiet, sheltered anchorage the family is again in happy mood. Before they forget all the bad bits, like the wet day and discomfort out at sea, the skipper thought it was time for a conference. Everyone was unanimous that it had been a wonderful holiday which they wanted to repeat — and in our own boat, the children clamoured. It wasn't easy to bring them back to reality. Once all their savings had been used to buy a boat, there would be no money for any other sort of holiday and they would probably have to make other economies as well. It wouldn't be all play either, the family would have to give up some time during the Easter holidays to help with the fitting out and this would mean quite a lot of hard, dirty work, (see Part 5). Anyhow, the skipper adds, it will probably take some time to find the right boat at a price they can afford, but perhaps there would be no harm in starting to look around. I would hazard a guess that as they drink a toast — in whisky or Coca-cola according to age — they all have a vague feeling that a new way of life is very definitely in the offing.

Part 4

The Floating Home

The General Layout

It is time at last to have a look at the sort of boat in which the Smiths have spent the last fortnight and I suggest that to get some idea of size you measure out on the lawn an area 21 ft long by 7½ ft wide. That is about the effective living area you will get in a boat that will be described technically as a 4½ tonner, 24 ft in length, the smallest yacht which, whatever the designers may claim, will provide an adequate home for four adults. The difference between the 24 ft overall length, to get used to the correct terms, and the 21 ft of effective living space is accounted for largely by the shape of the bow which, as you probably know, is canoe shaped and has an overhang.

Next, in the conventional type of layout you cut off 6 ft at each end. At the after end, this is taken up by the cockpit from which you work the boat and where it is hoped most of the crew will spend their time in good weather. There are boats with smaller cockpits, but it is uncomfortable if there is not room for everybody to sit outside when they want to.

The 6 ft at the forward end is the forecabin — it used to be called the forecastle in the old days of paid crews and a low, dark, smelly hole it could be too. In modern yachts, however, it is designed to provide a snug little cabin with two berths forming a vee shape. The sleeper's feet protrude into the overhang to give a little extra length. This forecabin may be partly partitioned off by a bulkhead — a strengthening piece of wall across the boat to help support the weight of the mast, with a door or curtain to fill the gap.

Our oblong box, therefore, if we shape it a little to resemble a boat, will be looking something like the schematic plan on page 78, and into the main cabin measuring about 9 ft by 7½ the builder has to fit:

Two 6 ft 2 in. berths
A dining table and general living space for four
Toilet compartment with some degree of privacy
Galley, including cooking space and working area
Chart table not less than 2 ft 4 in. by 1 ft 8 in. — the smallest area which will take an Admiralty chart with only one fold
Hanging clothes locker for go-ashore clothes
Hanging locker for four sets of wet oilskins
Storage for food, drink, clothes, sails, navigational equipment, ship's gear, tools, spare parts, etc. etc.

And if you think that by the time you have got all that into a 24 ft boat, there won't be room for the crew, let me assure you that we lived on such a boat with two more adults for four consecutive summers, including a six-

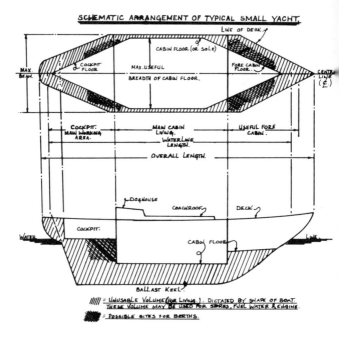

SCHEMATIC ARRANGEMENT OF TYPICAL SMALL YACHT.

LINE OF DECK

CABIN FLOOR (OR SOLE)

FORE CABIN FLOOR

COCKPIT FLOOR

MAX. USEFUL
BREADTH OF CABIN FLOOR.

MAX. BEAM.

CENTRE LINE (£)

COCKPIT.
MAIN WORKING
AREA.

MAIN CABIN
LIVING.

WATERLINE LENGTH.

USEFUL FORE
CABIN.

OVERALL LENGTH.

DOGHOUSE

COACHROOF

DECK

COCKPIT.

WATER

CABIN FLOOR

LINE

BALLAST KEEL.

////// = UNUSABLE VOLUME (FOR LIVING.) DICTATED BY SHAPE OF BOAT.
THESE VOLUME MAY BE USED FOR STORES, FUEL WATER & ENGINE.

███ = POSSIBLE SITES FOR BERTHS.

week cruise along the French coast, when we lost the mast off Cap Gris Nez in a force 7, pottered round the French canals and returned across the Channel in thick fog. Because we had studied some of the problems of living in a confined space, there wasn't a cross word as far as I remember and we were even then getting to the time of life when you get a little set in your ways.

But looking at the problem quite impartially there really are a surprising number of different ways you can fit the necessary impedimenta into the restricted space of a 24 ft boat.

Admittedly when I think back, we did find that there were one or two things on the list which we couldn't fit in. We had no hanging clothes locker, which does not matter much in these days of synthetic materials and casual dress; only men's jackets, if they insist on keeping one aboard for going ashore, really need hanging space. What was more serious I remember was that we had no chart table and had to manage on the dining table. This would be difficult on a long cruise, but if you are mainly pottering up and down the coast, you will find you can manage on your first boat.

Even without these two items *Jerboeen*, our 24 ft Mapleleaf looked a bit cramped because there were far fewer small boats in those days. I remember one day on the Somme, when we invited the lock-keeper, who had shown us a good mooring, aboard for a drink. She arrived with an enormous bunch of flowers from the garden and sat down at the table, saying *Santé* politely every time she raised her glass of cognac to her lips. She kept looking round in a puzzled sort of way until she could contain her curiosity no longer.

'Please,' she asked, 'where do you all sleep?'

We will now give you a number of alternative answers to that.

The Open Plan Layout
Even in these days of standard moulded boats you can still have a lot of fun and add your own idea of home comforts if you get in touch with the yard fitting a wooden inside to the shell. Often the boatyard will offer standard alternative lay-outs anyway and you will find

the builder is probably quite ready to include your own ideas if they are not too expensive.

It will always be a bit of a jigsaw puzzle and at the end there will be a few things for which you can't really find a place. In many boats the thing sacrificed first is stowage space. To us this seems a great mistake. Everybody will be uncomfortable if they have insufficient room to stow their personal possessions, while life will become irritating if you have had to leave out some of the gear and equipment which make life easier, even if they are not essential. There are boats on the market of only 19 ft, advertised as four berthers and boats of 24 ft claiming that there is room for five. If you take my advice you will have a jolly good look at these claims. There may be four or more berths, but there is nowhere to stow even a minimum suit of sails, or warps or spare anchors, and no chain locker or stowage for extended cruising. I have always wanted to go to the Boat Show with a trailer-load

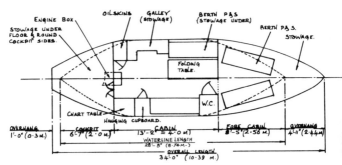

PLAN "A"
"CONVENTIONAL" ARRANGEMENT.

of the stuff which we have found vital on a long cruise and challenge some designers to fit it all into their shining dream boats. The trouble is, designers of mass produced small cruisers haven't got to go to sea in them for more than a demonstration cruise.

To return to our jigsaw puzzle, let me now try to describe some of the possible solutions; the most obvious is that shown in PLAN A.

Two berths can be fitted in up forward and two more in the main cabin, one on each side, while still leaving room for the toilet at the end of one berth and the galley behind the other. In this plan, just to make it clearer, we have shown a rather larger boat which has enabled us to get in an oilskin-locker and hanging cupboard as well. In our 24 ft boat, however, the cabin will be 4 ft shorter and will not extend much beyond the end of the starboard berth, leaving only a tiny galley and no hanging or oilskin-lockers. So we need to think again to see if we cannot make better use of our limited space.

Alternative arrangements of berths A dinette arrangement is the most common space saver, the table converting to a double berth at night. It was this which had mystified Michelle, the lock keeper, who had only been able to count two berths; she hadn't spotted that the table could just be lowered to create a double berth and even when we explained this she still needed some convincing that the resulting bed was large enough for two hefty adults. The popularity of the dinette, incidentally, is one sign of the growth of family cruising. A double berth would have been unthinkable in the days, not so long ago, when the wife was left at home while her husband went off for a jolly time with the boys.

A second possibility is to extend a single berth backwards into the cockpit, the legs going down into a sort of tunnel under the deck. These quarter berths, as they are called, have one advantage. They are comfortable on a long sea passage because the occupant is so closely hemmed in that there is no room to roll about. Some people find them claustrophobic, however, and many quarter berths require some agility to get in and out of them. A more serious disadvantage is that the berth encroaches on cockpit stowage space, a matter on which some skippers have strong views.

A third possibility, and indeed the only answer in very small boats is to bring the cockpit into the living space by rigging a canvas tent over the boom. It takes a bit of time night and morning and the berths may be a little short, but many a young family has started this way while the children were small.

We have also seen an extra berth squeezed in forward for the family by filling in the gap in the vee at nights.

Alternative positions for galley and toilet This arrangement of berths makes two other changes possible as shown on PLAN B

You will notice that as one side of the main cabin is now free the galley has been given more space along this side instead of being restricted to its little pen. This placing of the galley is also found on many much larger boats, though in our opinion it has grave disadvantages from the point of view of the poor old cook, who can only work by standing in the passage, right in the way of anybody moving to and fro, and has nowhere to get

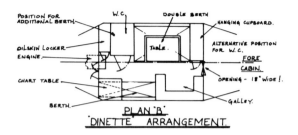

POSITION FOR ADDITIONAL BERTH

W.C.

DOUBLE BERTH

HANGING CUPBOARD.

OILSKIN LOCKER

ENGINE.

TABLE.

ALTERNATIVE POSITION FOR W.C.

FORE CABIN.

CHART TABLE

OPENING - 18" WIDE !.

BERTH.

GALLEY.

PLAN 'B'
DINETTE ARRANGEMENT.

wedged in if trying to cook out at sea.

With three berths (the double and a quarter berth) in the main cabin, there is a possibility of getting the toilet out of the way by shifting it forward to the alternative position shown on Plan B on one side of the forecabin, and indeed in many small boats this is the only place where it is possible to squeeze it in. During the day, indeed, the toilet is not badly placed up forward; it is just unfortunate, assuming the one forecabin berth is occupied, if someone has a tummy upset in the middle of the night!

Drying wet oilskins   Even though in 24 ft there will be no room for a separate oilskin-locker, some provision must be made for drying the pile which will be dumped on the floor at the end of a wet passage. It does not matter if they drip onto the floor, because the water will drain away into the bilges, but they must be kept from dripping over berths and sleeping bags. An additional advantage of moving one berth from the forecabin is to provide a little wall space where the oilskins can hang — if necessary behind the toilet.

83

Improvements possible in a larger boat   By the end of four years you may not only have decided cruising is really part of your chosen way of life but you may be getting more ambitious and feel that for longer cruises you need a little more space than we have been discussing. I am sure, if you can afford it, you will also be wanting something with more headroom than 4 ft 9 in. Indeed the little *Mapleleaf* had done us proud on our return to cruising in this country and while we decided what we really wanted for a final boat, which would have to be a compromise between what we could afford in retirement and our ideas of comfort, while retaining a good sailing machine for long foreign cruises, so we ordered off the drawing board her bigger sister the *Oakleaf.* She was only 4 ft longer, but what a difference 4 ft can make! With the same basic layout, we now had room for two hanging lockers — one for go-ashore clothes in the forecabin and the other for oilskins by the door, the only sensible place to avoid walking right through the cabin in dripping clothes. It was possible to include a chart table over one end of the single berth in the main cabin (we now had a five berth boat) and our friends, if they wished to be private, could shut the sliding door across the forecabin. Best of all, we had room for a separate enclosed toilet. It is true it is a little small and that when in use, it encroaches onto the passage, thus preventing movement from main to fore cabin, but it does provide some privacy and by a cunning arrangement of doors it can be shut off from either side, or from both at once. Before we show you some photographs of the inside, we must still look at one or two other arrangements.

The Central Cockpit Layout

After looking at the plans, you will appreciate that in any small boat, privacy is a relative matter, particularly as partitions are thin and anything but soundproof. Those who are worried about living at close quarters and treasure their privacy, particularly at night, may like to consider an alternative layout in which the cockpit is moved to the middle of the boat, to make space for an after cabin. In the smaller versions the layout is shown in PLAN C below.

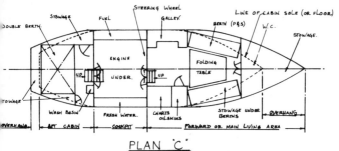

PLAN 'C'

CENTRE COCKPIT

In larger versions of the centre cockpit boat the forward end will be divided into main and fore cabins with layouts similar to those we have just been discussing. The attraction of this layout is that the after cabin provides secluded sleeping quarters for two and in the larger versions may form a self-contained suite complete with its own toilet, wash basin and even shower. In small boats, entry to the after cabin will be by a companion way from the cockpit. In bigger boats,

85

nearing the gin palace class, there will probably be a connecting passage under the wheelhouse floor or side deck.

However, we are thinking now of the normal smallish family cruiser and we must look at the disadvantages of a layout which at first sight is attractive. Everything on a small boat is a compromise and if you gain in one direction you have to sacrifice something elsewhere. In this case there may be two areas more cramped than in the conventional layout, the cockpit and the main cabin. The latter is particularly important because it will still have to provide living and eating space for the whole crew, plus berths for two or four, plus the essential extras like galley, toilet and chart table and all this in a space at least 7 ft less than before because of the after cabin.

So, you take your choice — greater comfort and privacy at night or a roomier cabin for the various daytime activities. The decision may depend on your family or the sort of friends with whom you expect to cruise.

The Modern Solutions to the Space Problem : The Catamaran and the Trimaran

Before we leave the question of layout, we must look at the latest and most revolutionary of ideas. The catamaran, as you will know, is a boat with two hulls connected by a bridge deck. We shall have more to say about it as a sailing machine in Part V so here we will just concentrate on its accommodation possibilities. The living room, or saloon, will be on the bridge deck and usually consists of little but a table surrounded by a U-shaped settee. In a four berth 'Cat' there will probably be

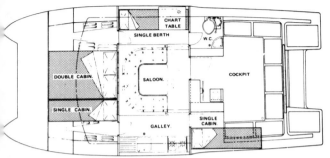

The layout of a 9 metre Catamaran

room for six or eight people to sit round the table in comfort and enjoy the view. This is one of the advantages of the catamaran over the normal boat, in which the cabin is usually too low to see out of the portholes without standing up. Indeed in the saloon of the cat you can't stand up — the roof cannot be raised enough to give standing headroom without increasing windage problems. It does not matter so much because all the work is done down in the hulls, which are reached by steps from both sides of the saloon. Here there is plenty of headroom and plenty of space, which can be divided up as you like to provide a number of separate *single* cabins, a luxury in a small boat, to give the cook elbow room or to provide stowage for practically everything you might think of bringing aboard. There will be a separate, enclosed toilet and a roomy one by ship's standards. In addition some catamarans have a double cabin on the bridge deck forward of the saloon which itself can always provide a couple of extra berths if needed. At the same time both cockpit and the foredeck are so large that you

The galley of a 9 metre Catalac inside the port hull shows the difference in level between saloon and hulls

could dance on them — certainly the modern jig about variety.

In the trimaran the accommodation plan is more like that of the conventional yacht, as the two outer hulls are not part of the living space, but the width of this type of multi-hull boat does naturally mean a more spacious cabin than in normal boats of the same length.

Creating a home

We have already introduced you briefly to *Kala Sona* —

The Main Cabin — Crew relaxing after the Day's Sail. Note 1. the opening brass scuttle (between the clock and barometer) — you really need two in each cabin. 2. The sink and galley offset to port, so cookie is not obstructing the passage through. 3. Removable table, with fiddles, which gives way to a double berth at night. 4. Sliding door is opened to show fore cabin and the heads are between cabins on starboard side.

the name, incidentally, means 'Little Singing Duck' in Syriac, as I was writing a book on the Assyrians when she was being built. Now, we would like to take you down below to look at her more closely and let us show you all the refinements that have been added over the years to ensure comfortable living and a cosy home. I only wish we could have included colour photographs here because in black and white it is difficult to convey the feeling of warmth which comes from the cabin walls, cut out of solid pieces of beautiful African mahogany. It is purely a matter of personal taste whether you prefer to live in a warm, cosily coloured wooden boat or try and create the same effect by kitting out the inside of a GRP boat in wood. We like wooden boats and ten years ago it was still possible to have one built. Today you would probably have to buy second hand unless fairly well off, but many boat builders are lavish with wooden linings and fittings inside a glass reinforced plastic hull to improve the inside appearance.

Even with our lovely pieces of wood, we don't like bare walls. The ship's clock and the barometer which you will see above the dining table are normal and essential equipment on any boat, though the clock is larger than you would expect to find on a small yacht. We just happen to like to see it from the cockpit. Below them you will notice two semi-circular wooden objects. These are ash trays, simply wooden bowls sawn in half, the open side covered in marine ply and mounted on a hinged bracket for emptying. We think they look pleasant and they have the advantage that they cannot be knocked over. We keep the matches handy too — there are two boxes under that little embroidered cover sent to us by a Danish boy who joined us on one trip. You will notice that there is a useful shelf in the middle which takes things like the transistor radio, binoculars and bridge cards and small cupboards for personal items on each side made in a contrasting wood with inlaid edges for effect. These are all things which you would expect to find, but you may be a little more surprised to see that we also have pictures on the walls. We do not have bare walls at home; we didn't see why we should not have pictures aboard too and thought that some Italian wooden inlay work looked rather good against the mahogany.

On the opposite side we have our bookshelf, containing a mixture of navigational tomes, bird, flower and butterfly books and general reading. Aft of this is the chart table which goes over part of the single berth and also has to hold the ship-to-shore radio and has a shallow chart locker beneath it. By raising the radio an inch off the table we can use an Admiralty chart with only one fold; it is difficult to find room for a full sized chart table on a 27 ft boat. Above we produce another of our surprises — two flower vases. Again, why not? The vases slip into holders screwed on to the walls and it is surprising what a colourful display you can get with a wild flower collection from the hedgerows near most anchorages.

Finally, in your first look round, you will have noticed the furnishings — a carpet and curtains. There are some people who regard a carpet in a boat as horribly un-nautical, but it is a comfort when you get out of bed on a cold morning and helps to keep the feet warm at other times. We have found that rubber-backed synthetic carpet is the best and at last we have found a wavy design in brown and fawn which does not even show East Coast mud! Curtains are accepted as a necessity to give privacy for washing and dressing when moored close to other boats and we could not see why they had to be drab, sober affairs, so we found a pretty rose pattern and used it for some of the cushion covers too.

Domestic life

A comfortable night's sleep

You will soon discover when you start to do any jobs aboard that a boat has not got a single straight line. This means that you cannot just go and pick up a mattress anywhere; berth cushions have to be made to fit the individual boat. Unless you like a spartan life, you should be suspicious of any claim that a three-inch cushion is enough. Four inches is the minimum for comfort, remembering that the cushion will not have a spring base underneath — it will be on top of hard boards.

Most berth cushions are foam filled with a vinyl covering and our friends assure us that they are very comfortable on their four-inch cushions and do not envy us our extra touch of luxury — six-inch Dunlopillo, which we think is worth the extra cost.

If you have started by chartering, you will probably find that the berths are equipped with sheets and blankets and indeed, if you want them there is no objection to ordinary bedclothes, particularly in any separate cabins which are not part of the general living quarters. But blankets are difficult to stow away tidily during the day and we have actually come across few boats where they are used. Most of us find that sleeping bags are easier and warmer. For boat use, a synthetic filling is more suitable than down because the former dries more quickly if, by mischance, it should get wet and the 38 oz. weight is the minimum you need to keep warm. If you happen to live afloat early in the season — and for the last year or two we have been having heavy frosts at night in May — you may need a blanket as well for the first trip.

Whether or not you use a sheet inner to the sleeping bag is a matter of taste. It would be nice to have one for very hot weather when the sleeping bag gets a bit sweaty, but for the rest of the time many of us find it an unnecessary nuisance. It is difficult enough to struggle into one sleeping bag, let alone two, so we just tell our friends that if they want an inner they should bring their own — we can't provide them.

We keep one ordinary pillow aboard for each berth and have a cover for it, matching the curtains, to keep it clean and tidy during the day. In addition there are a number of cushions for the cockpit and deck use which come into service as under pillows for those who want them.

Washing facilities and the fresh water supply
In any small yacht washing facilities will be primitive, limited mainly to the sink or washing-up bowl, but it is useful if space permits to add to these by fitting a small folding basin in the heads.

In any case, fresh water for washing will be in limited supply. Our tank holds about 20 gal., about average capacity for the size of boat and in addition we keep a reserve of 5 gal. in cans, a safety precaution so that we can never actually run dry without warning. Again this is a swings and roundabout matter. We carry 28 gal. of diesel fuel to save having to find a bowser in a foreign harbour too often but some prefer to reduce the fuel tanks and increase the water capacity. We find 20 gal. should last four people about five days at sea, which is all most families like at a stretch before finding a harbour.

If, as we have said, you are spending each night in

yacht harbours, filling the tank is no trouble; there will be a water point and hose on the pontoon. In an area where there are no yacht harbours it is a different matter. Then you can fill up only by rowing ashore with the cans and finding the nearest tap. In some places this may entail quite a walk with heavy cans and the water may look a little suspect in the more remote parts such as the west coast of Scotland, and some places abroad. I remember one day on the French canals when our tank was getting low and, finding that the hamlet where we had tied up had no obvious water supply, we put our problem to the oldest inhabitant who was sitting on a bank.

'You wish for water?' he says, regarding the canal with a faint air of surprise.

'*Eau potable*', we explain.

It evidently takes him a long time and quite a sustained mental effort to hoist in the fact that the mad Englishmen actually want to drink the stuff but his face lights up eventually.

'There used to be a well, a good well; now let me see, *ça va* I know, just to the north of the village old Madame Bontemps garden. Tell her I sent you and she will let you have some.'

We explain that we are not very good at wells and are really looking for a *robinet* if possible. His face shows his real concern for us and he hastens to say.

'A *robinet*? No I would not advise it. The water comes from you do not know where and nowadays they put into it, you do not know what. But a well now, you know where you are; that is good water, it has some taste to it and it comes up from the good earth — that is how it should be!'

94

Heating, lighting and ventilation

In most yachts where the auxiliary motor is used infrequently, electricity is likely to be in short supply because batteries will not be charged often enough. In a motor boat where a powerful engine is in use every time you move, it is a different matter, as indeed it may be if you are cruising from one marina to another and know that you can plug in to the mains supply as soon as you tie up. It is even said that in some American marinas the electric lead is rushed ashore before the boat is tied up.

The use of the main alternative to electricity, gas, is one of the most controversial matters in the yachting world. There are some skippers who will not have it aboard at any price; there is one country, too — Sweden — where it is banned on the grounds that it is too dangerous and causes too many accidents. The danger is that if there is a leak, the gas (which sinks because it is heavier than air) cannot escape. In a caravan it will get away through the floorboards, but in a boat it goes straight down to the bilges where it cannot escape — until someone lights a match!

Despite the worries, however, there are thousands of yachtsmen using propane or butane gas without any worry, provided they observe one or two simple precautions. First, the bottle from which the supply is being drawn *must not* be in the cabin. It should be outside in the cockpit and in a locker which is not airtight. Secondly, the gas should always be turned off at the mains when not in use. It is the last job every night and it should be the duty of the washer-up to turn it off after each meal. If the skipper is still worried it is possible to instal a gas detector.

If you cannot produce enough electricity and the skipper will not permit gas, you have to fall back on oil or meths. There are plenty of cookers and heaters available using both and there is no light more soft and attractive than that from an oil lamp. The difficulty is that in a small boat, oil lamps have to be gimballed so that they swing with the movement of the boat and these gimballed lamps take up space. We would have liked to have them in *Kala Sona* but could find nowhere to put them where they wouldn't be knocked every time someone moved about.

Our own arrangements are a reasonable compromise. Cooking and the main cabin lighting are by gas. The strip lights, as you will have noticed from the photographs, take up very little space. In addition we have a small gas heater which screws onto the top of a Camping Gaz cylinder which is a joy on a really cold day — so far as we know Calor gas does not make anything similar. We do however have supplementary electric lights in the three places where they may be needed at night after the gas has been turned off—the forecabin, the heads and over the chart table in the main cabin for long passages.

The refrigerator is electric — the gas model necessitated leaving the gas on when we did not want it — and we use electricity too for an extractor fan in the heads, which brings us to the last problem — ventilation, which in many modern boats is inadequate because they are built without anything that opens except the cabin door and a hatch. However many roof ventilators you have, they are no adequate substitute for open windows on a hot day. A fore hatch helps and gives a chance of a through draught so long as it is dry, but on a hot, wet, thundery night you may have to shut both hatch and cabin door while the cabin gets more and more intolerable.

We decided that we did not want to be cooped up in an airless space so when we had *Kala Sona* built we insisted on opening portholes, on both sides, in both the main cabin and the forecabin. They were expensive but we still think they were worth the money. In the galley we have a sliding window, which was cheaper than a porthole. If the rain is too heavy, however, even the portholes have to be closed because of the splash from the side decks and in these conditions we have one other dodge, which you may like to copy to enable you to leave the cabin door open without the rain driving in. We have a piece of canvas made with four good eyelet holes and tie two above the after hatch, and two to each edge of the cockpit. This provides a sort of porch over the door to enable air but not rain to get to the main cabin.

The dining table

In many boats the day cabin is spoilt by a fixed dining table. It cuts down space both for walking about and for pre-dinner entertaining. With small children aboard the fixed table tends to be a nightmare because on a wet day it leaves them with virtually no floor space for play.

Sometimes this inflexibility in the cabin arrangements is inescapable. In boats with a centre board, for example, (see Part 5) the construction may demand an immovable central obstruction to which the table is fixed. I do suspect however, that there are some designers who do not think enough about the problems of *living* when afloat and that if pressed they might come up with an idea that suits you better than the original design.

97

In *Kala Sona*, for example, the problem of floor space has been solved by having a folding and easily stowable table on two metal legs which screw into a solid floor beam. The gap in the middle is filled at night by a sliding slatted support which disappears under the side cushion during the day. This arrangement has the additional advantage that, unlike many dinettes, we can sit round all four sides of the table — a great help when playing bridge!

How to provide good food with the minimum of effort
There is no reason why you should not feed just as well aboard as at home. It is more a question of good catering than good cooking and of adapting your ideas to suit the conditions under which you will have to work. Before we talk about the menus, however, we might take a closer look at

The galley   We have already mentioned our preference for the 'pen' type of galley and as you will see from the photograph, ours is a nice little box where the cook can wedge herself comfortably and yet be out of everybody's way. At the forward end, the sink with fresh and salt water pumps and draining board are attached to the back of the double berth and together measure about 2 ft by 1. There is a sink cover for increasing the working area and under the draining board there is room for a small fridge. At the end of the draining board there is a little cupboard containing everything needed for hot drinks, so that anybody can make one without having to grope in the

The Offset Galley. Showing dresser (for pewter mugs and melaware cups), wine glass cupboard, engine casing (on which the cook sits) and between it and the calor gas stove with its two burners and a grill, is a three tier trash bin, plate cupboard and detachable cutlery drawer on top — and, as elsewhere a picture — why not? It is our home for much of the summer.

main stowage. At right angles to the sink there is the small cooker, a standard two-burner and grill gas cooker measuring about 16 in. by 12 in. and underneath there is extensive stowage going back nearly 2 ft to the side of the boat. The lower part is used for pots and pans, the upper for food, and with this sort of cupboard it pays to be methodical and know exactly where everything is, otherwise you will continually be unpacking and repacking. It is for this reason too that I discourage anybody else from going to this cupboard. One's dearest friends will make chaos!

The third side of the box is made up by the wall that separates the cabin from the cockpit and on this above the galley we have our home-made dresser, containing cocktail glasses, pewter beer mugs and Melaware cups, with at the bottom a tiny cupboard for toilet things such as toothbrushes and razor. On the floor to the left of the galley we keep the cutlery and plates in another piece of furniture of our own design. The cutlery box is at the top and lifts out to give access to the plate rack, holding twelve plates and four bowls. And finally at the back of the galley there is a comfortably large wooden seat over the engine. It is bigger than would be normal in a boat our size (see Part 5) and it does take up space, but it is an extremely comfortable seat when you want to watch the pots and pans and it is also the best seat in the boat on a wet day if you don't want to be in the cockpit. You can see out of the dog-house windows and — if the diesel has been running — it is deliciously warm.

Cookers Types of cookers — Calor gas, paraffin or meths — have already been mentioned. The choice is largely a matter of taste but I would suggest that you are limiting yourself unnecessarily if you chose one without a grill. An oven is a different matter. There are plenty of small gas stoves available complete with an oven, but to accommodate it you have to give up precious food storage space, or have your cooking burners inconveniently high. There are some folding ovens on the market but I don't think they are worth the trouble, and a pressure cooker acts as a substitute. For keeping food hot just use an enamel plate covered with a saucepan lid, above a saucepan of boiling water or the vegetables.

Kitchen utensils Everyone will have their own ideas, but my list consists of:

    1 large pressure cooker with an additional separate lid, so that it can do double duty as a large saucepan.

    1 large, heavy iron frying pan with a 9 in. base and 12 in. top.

    3 saucepans of 4, $2^1/_2$ and 2 pt. capacities, all of course with lids.

    2 bowls, one enamel and the other plastic, fulfilling a variety of purposes from mixing bowl to spare soup plate.

    1 large chopping board measuring 21 in. by 7 in. This board has a second function; it is large enough for the back to be used as a bosun's chair.

    A collection of asbestos mats for use not only on the cooker but to protect the varnish on those occasions when I run out of space and need to park a hot pan outside the galley area.

    In addition I keep aboard an egg whisk, a mouli cheese grater and a wall can opener and I have recently added a steamer, which doubles the capacities of the largest saucepan. Colander, wooden spoon, bread knife, sharp kitchen knife and a slip for sharpening the knife complete the list.

    You may be surprised at one omission from this list — a kettle, because it takes up too much space to stow. Water can be boiled just as well in a saucepan with a lid, and as often as not it is the enamel plate keeping food hot which does duty as the lid. We don't bother with a teapot

Starboard Side of Cabin. Showing library (with retaining bar), drop-head wall ashtray, medicine case, courtesy ensigns, etc; chart table, chart cupboard and ship to shore Radio transmitter — and a vase for wild flowers!

either, another item which takes up a disproportionate amount of space, and using tea bags, tea can be made just as well directly in a cup. I admit that we might feel differently about this if we had a passion for tea drinking!

There is one other limitation on cooking activities. The cooker is not only small, but the area is further limited by its fiddles — surrounding rails to prevent pots from sliding off. Anyone intending to cook much at sea may also need gimbals to keep the pots upright. This will reduce the space even more but even with fiddles, I find I cannot use the large saucepan and frying pan at the same time. This is one point to bear in mind when getting your

The Boat is also your summer home so give some thought to making your cockpit a comfortable place in which to dine or just entertain friends after the day's sail. Folding glass or mug holders and a 'slot-in' table are a good start. Here we are celebrating arrival at the hospitable Royal Netherlands Yacht Club after a rough night passage to Ijmuiden.

equipment. Another is to ensure that it all fits one inside the other for economy in stowage space.

Finally there is a collection of airtight, plastic containers for stores such as flour, sugar, salt and rice as well as for biscuits and cheese.

Some catering suggestions I imagine that most people on holiday don't attempt to cook more than twice a day — a good breakfast and good evening meal, with a picnic-type lunch wherever it is eaten. What is more, in the restricted conditions of a boat or a caravan or a camp, the cook will be well advised to restrict the cooked part of any meal to one course. For puddings, the family will be just as happy with cake and fruit, or the wide range of excellent ready made tarts now available. In buying cakes do remember that anything brittle or squashy will be impossible to store; you soon learn to recognise those which can be thrown into the back of a locker and come out unspoilt!

For the rest I usually plan my menus in five-day groups. We do not go ashore to shop more often than necessary, but after five days we need to fill up with water if not with food. With a young and hungry family demanding quantities of bread, it may be difficult to last out for the full five days unless storage space is generous. In most boats, however, it is unlikely that there will be a large enough refrigerator (if there is one at all) to produce fresh meat on all five days. For the last two the store of tinned and dried foods will come into use for concocting various dishes.

Two typical five days menus might therefore consist of:

Day 1 (Shopping Day)	Lamb chops	Pork chops
Day 2	Roast beef (pot roast in pressure cooker)	Irish stew
Day 3	Soup and cold beef	Chicken casserole
Day 4	Curry (remains of beef, if any, or tin)	Chicken or kidney risotto
Day 5	Spaghetti Bolognese (with minced beef if any, or tin)	Cauliflower cheese or Welsh rarebit (if enough bread)

These menus have been selected because there is no dish there which takes more than 30 minutes to prepare; for most of them 20 minutes is enough. The actual cooking time may of course be longer than that and, particularly if cooking by gas, you will have to keep an eye on it to make sure that a low gas does not blow out or that the pressure cooker doesn't go off pressure, but you can at least get on with other jobs or amuse yourself in your own way while the meal is cooking. There is one thing about the confined space on a boat — it is not difficult to cook and join in general activities or conversation at the same time!

Most of you will not need any instructions on cooking the dishes listed above, so I will confine myself to a few quick hints.

Pot roast of beef	For those unaccustomed to a pressure cooker, I suggest that the best joints are rolled ribs or rolled brisket. A good butcher will advise, but do avoid topside: it's too dry.
Curry	If you like it you will have your own recipe. If you don't I suggest substituting a hotpot with the remains of the beef, perhaps a tin of stewed steak and tinned or fresh vegetables to taste.
Spaghetti Bolognese	You can buy the sauce in tins or packets, but without much effort you can make a better version of your own using chopped onion and bacon and tins of savoury minced steak and tomatoes — the 6–8 oz. sizes are large enough for four You can add any odd bits of vegetable such as grated carrot, chopped celery or green pepper that you have about, and may need a little stock.

I do not pressure cook the spaghetti; this is one of the dishes where the pressure cooker is used as a large saucepan. After draining the spaghetti return it to the pan with a good knob of butter, about two tablespoonfuls of grated cheese (you will of course have plenty more to sprinkle on top) and a little of the sauce. Mix well together and reheat before serving.

Pork Chops   I always keep a tin or two of apple sauce in the store. It is one of the tins worth taking with you because it is not always easy to find.

Chicken casserole   For this I use frozen chicken, partly because it will be a day or two after shopping before it is even ready to cook. It can be pressure cooked, but I prefer it boiled. Put into cold water, bring slowly to the boil, simmer for 45 minutes and cool in the liquid. I cook the chicken the day before then joint it and for this casserole mix with tins of sweetcorn, peas and red peppers. With a hungry family I would add some potatoes.

Risotto   The easiest method I have found of cooking rice is the Egyptian. Measure the rice carefully in a cup (a teacupful is enough for two), fry it for a few minutes, then add the *same quantity* of water or stock as of rice. Bring to the boil, boil hard for two minutes, then turn the heat down as low as possible, put on a lid and leave for twenty minutes. At the end of that time the rice should be cooked and all the liquid absorbed.

To go with it you can prepare any mixture you like — say fried onion and bacon, chicken pieces or tinned braised kidneys, mushrooms and other

	vegetables. A little stock or sauce may be needed
Cauliflower cheese	Only one suggestion here, that you brighten it up by adding a little fried chopped bacon, a few sliced tomatoes and, if you have it, some sliced cooked potato. It all helps to make the dish more solid as well as tastier.

One last thought, particularly for those who are used to popping round the corner to the supermarket every day. Do make a shopping list, you will not be popular if you get back aboard and find you have forgotten the butter.

Clothes

It is no good thinking that you are going to look smart or glamorous on a boat, that is if you are going to be a member of the crew and not just a passenger. All you need for day wear is shirt, slacks and jerseys plus underwear to taste. For long cruises there are many who reckon that on night passages it is so cold you want to be thoroughly old fashioned and go for 'long johns' or wear pyjamas under your trousers. For climbing about on deck it is much more comfortable if slacks are not too tight, particularly round the knees; besides, there are occasions when one needs to roll them up. Smart, slinky models are unsuitable for anybody except a passenger and pockets are a must. A woman can't take a handbag with her if she goes forward to pick up a mooring but she may need one or two small tools, or pieces of string — apart from a handkerchief! Apart from this the most vital thing is to have plenty of thick heavy jerseys. The normal rather loosely knitted garment, even in a quick knit, is just not warm enough and it is well worth going to a yacht chandlers to find the right sort of oiled wool thick jersey. Then you can pile on some of your older ordinary jerseys underneath, and with a layer of about three you will probably be warm on most passages. You must of course take one change of clothes even if you are only going for a weekend, in case you get wet or even fall in, and if you are aboard for any length of time two changes is desirable.

You also probably need something tidier for the occasions when you go ashore, and if you want to frequent smart yacht clubs, the men may feel undressed if they are not in the fashion with a reefer jacket. But in many parts of the coast most of us get by simply by keeping one pair of slacks relatively clean and finding a clean shirt or tunic top to go with them. For women it is much easier than it used to be now that one can go practically anywhere in slacks and thank goodness, too, for drip-dry clothes. In a crisis you can always wash something out aboard and hang it up in the rigging to dry.

For normal foot gear aboard you must have a pair of proper yachting shoes made with a special non-skid sole. Ordinary tennis shoes are not good enough and whatever you wear you need shoes without heels, which are liable to catch. For going ashore you can wear something smarter, but it is kinder to the boat if you choose something with a soft sole. In no circumstances should any woman go aboard with a high heel that may damage the. decks.

Apart from normal clothes, everybody needs a good set of wet weather gear and this means a full set of 'oilies' (nowadays made of P.V.C.). The set consists of trousers and jacket, with either a hood on the jacket or a sou'wester — it's a matter of choice. These sets of waterproof clothing will not be cheap, because they are going to get hard wear and anything lightweight will tear too easily. But they are one of the essentials and are best bought from the specialist suppliers. Don't forget, incidentally, to allow for the thick jerseys underneath when trying on the jacket.

Finally you will need boots. The ordinary yachting half boot is the most comfortable but there seems to be a modern fashion for something a little bit longer. Ordinary wellingtons are not suitable — they tend to be a bit too tight in the leg and most of them are made with a heel.

First aid and the medicine chest

Once you are on the boat you are very much on your own. If anybody gets ill or hurt it may be hours, or even a day or so before there is any possibility of getting help and a good medical kit is therefore essential equipment. This should include a first-aid book and one of the crew, at least, should preferably have had some training.

Now I'm not going to try to list all the things you should carry; that is a job for the experts and you will find good lists in advanced books. But let me just outline briefly here the complaints for which adequate remedies must be available:

1. *Cuts.* Ranging from a tiny snick with a kitchen knife to a bad gash. For these you will need disinfectant and plenty of dressings of all sorts and sizes.

2. *Burns.* The modern first-aid book will tell you what is nowadays the approved treatment, but don't forget that burns may mean a bad case of sunburn as well.

109

Somehow people don't seem to realise how badly they're catching the sun in a cool sea breeze.

3. *Tummy upsets.* 'Stop-you-uppers' or 'loosen-you-up-pers' as somebody rather crudely puts it. You will no doubt have your own favourite remedy or your doctor will prescribe something suitable.

An eye bath and eye lotion, an ointment or lotion for insect bites and stings, insect repellant, gargle and your favourite cold cure are additional remedies which I like to keep aboard, but you will know best the sort of ailments from which your family is likely to suffer. In the event of a really bad accident or broken limb you should be able to find enough bits amongst the ship's gear to construct a splint, while scarves can be used to make a sling. Aspirins and pain-killers should be included and don't forget the seasick pills. Written down like this it does not seem a very long list but I can assure you that I have two cupboards full of medical equipment as well as spare bandages and dressings in a separate bag. Admittedly I have been lucky and have very rarely had to use them, but I would never leave any of them behind. You never know what is going to happen next when you get a boat.

One last thing, which needs no equipment, should be studied by everyone aboard: artificial respiration. You will probably never have to cope with a case of drowning but how terrible you would feel if you had no idea what to do.

Stowage

You may by now be a little tired of the word 'stowage,' and think I have an obsession with it. But after the first trip or two you will agree that no one can have a comfortable home without adequate space for the essentials. Life becomes irritating if things are left about because there is nowhere to put them away and it is equally irritating if you are always having to move one thing to get at something else behind it. So let us finish this part by taking another look round *Kala Sona* to see what we have to fit in and how we do it.

Most of the stowage in the cabins lies under the berths and up in the forecabin we put them as high as we could, while still allowing room to sit up in bed. The water tank is up here and so are the sails — one of the bulkiest items — with much vital equipment such as spare anchors, buoys, navigational equipment and tool bags. On each side a section of these lockers about 2 ft square has been cut off for clothes lockers. In the main cabin, the lockers under the berths, which are the daytime seats, are necessarily shallower and in shallow-draught boats may be difficult to keep dry, because when sailing and well heeled over, bilge water will slop up the sides. The lockers in these boats need lining with a cellophane sheet and, as an additional precaution, clothes are best stored in waterproof bags — they are in any case easier to find that way than all jumbled up.

The space under the berths is not the only available area for stowage. On most boats the cabin top does not extend to the side of the boat; there is a side deck about nine inches wide to enable the crew to go forward without climbing over the roof. Inside, this space under the side decks is invaluable for cupboards, and is where our bookshelf fits in, along with the small cupboards we showed you in the photograph of *Kala Sona*, and we get in two more in the forecabin in the space over the sleeper's feet. These cupboards, we think, are a vital addition to the main stowage for all the smaller personal possessions: toilet things, make-up, cameras, spare glasses, pipes and tobacco — the list is endless.

Once you live in a boat you will be surprised how many corners you will find where extra cupboards can be fitted in without getting in the way. For example, racks over the berths can be fitted into the space between the ceiling beams. You can't walk there so the loss of a few inches of headroom does not matter and it gives extra space for charts, large instruction books, chess board, writing board and anything else which can be stowed flat. Any trouble with condensation is solved by the use of cellophane bags. Finally, down below it is worth taking up the floor boards and looking at the bilges. It is not dry stowage; there is usually a little water in the bilges, so labels are inclined to float off after a time, but apart from this, unopened bottles and tins come to no harm and are mostly recognisable even without their labels. You can mark the tins with paint for a long cruise lasting several months, but it is really not necessary for the normal short cruise.

However clever you have been in using up every corner, you will be unusual if you do not sometimes complain of lack of space and you will have to be firm with your crews about their own luggage.

Even the most enchanting poppets must be told that suitcases cannot physically be crammed into clothes lockers! There is indeed only one group of owners who can sit back and gloat, watching the rest of us struggle — those whose chosen boat is a trimaran or a catamaran.

" ... *Even the most enchanting poppets must be told that suitcases cannot be crammed physically into the clothes lockers!*"

Rubbish disposal

In inland waterways and marinas there is no trouble; there are plenty of bins ashore and strict rules to prevent rubbish being thrown overboard. In tidal waters it is more difficult, if visits ashore are infrequent, to bury or burn it and a binful of waste food soon develops an intolerable smell. It is generally, therefore, regarded as permissible to put this type of waste overboard, provided it is done on the ebb when it will be carried out to sea. Much of it will sink at once and the rest should disappear fairly quickly with one exception — grapefruit halves, which float down until they ground on the bank below the mooring where they resist every effort of the tides to dislodge them! Empty bottles and tins can go overboard too, provided you ensure they sink; otherwise they will stay afloat indefinitely and may damage somebody's propellor. To ensure sinking, tins must have holes at both ends and bottles must be filled.

In disposing of rubbish, there is one golden rule. *NEVER put any plastic material overboard*. It will neither sink nor disintegrate. What is worse, the larger and longer pieces have an uncanny knack of finding a nice propeller to wrap themselves round, with consequences that will soon be well known to you.

Part 5

Owning a Boat

The type of boat

Defining your requirements

Every boat is a compromise, because in seeking our ideal most of us are trying to combine incompatible elements. We would like a boat large enough for a fast, comfortable sea passage and small enough to explore shallow creeks or anchor in tiny island harbours; a boat that is both an efficient sailing machine and a comfortable home; a boat large enough to take all the family and friends in comfort but small enough for husband and wife to manage on their own if the family has better things to do.

For most of us the ideal does not exist and we shall get near it only if we start with some hard thinking about the sort of cruising we want to do and our concept of what life should be when afloat. In other words we need to establish our priorities and to help in doing so, we suggest you need to ask yourself the following questions:

Do you really want to make long sea passages?

If so, which are you going to enjoy most, the passages themselves or the places you hope to visit?

How keen are you on actual sailing, as distinct from just getting across the sea by the quickest and most comfortable method?

Where are you going to make your home port and what is the surrounding area like for weekend cruising?

What size crew do you expect to have?

Do you want to trail the boat home for the winter?

How much time are you prepared to spend on maintenance?

Do you enjoy pottering about and doing jobs aboard or not?

Only after you have thought out your answers will you be ready to make a number of fundamental decisions on the type of boat that will best meet your needs. The first of them is:

Power or Sail? The choice between
(a) Motor boats   As we mentioned earlier, cruising and sailing are not synonymous. There are plenty of people making long cruises in motor boats and there is no problem in doing so provided the boat has twin engines. For single-engine boats a long sea passage is dangerous, because if the engine develops a serious fault there may be nothing even a skilled engineer can do but sit and wallow until somebody finds him or hears his SOS. How many people take this risk can be gauged from the fact that the greater number of lifeboat calls from pleasure craft come from broken-down motor boats.

Cruising under power has both advantages and disadvantages. You will usually make much better speed than under sail. Indeed we have listened with appropriate awe at the bar of the Royal Temple Yacht Club in Ramsgate to gentlemen discussing 'popping over to Calais' for a drink, an hour's run we gathered, when it might take us about five or six. This curtailment of the sea passage might commend itself to some members of the family. But it is not only a very expensive way of going about it, but also one which gives, I would have thought, little pleasure in doing. You may make better progress against a moderate headwind, as you can point the boat closer to its direction, but you will be gale-bound like all other small boats when the wind is really strong. The living quarters are likely to be more spacious than in a similar-sized sailing yacht while the crew will have an easier time — there may be no instructions to go up on the foredeck to change sails in a rough sea but you will roll 'something 'orrible', so I hope you have a good stomach. On balance you may well prefer a motor boat if your object in cruising is to use the boat as a sort of nautical caravan, enjoying the life in British or foreign ports, with the chance of cruising among enchanting islands which you could never visit by car and caring little about the journey except to get it over as quickly as possible. It is also easier and more fun touring foreign canals in a motor boat because you will not have the problem of lowering the mast for bridges. The length of each sea passage will of course be limited by your fuel capacity; it will inescapably be more expensive, and sometimes a bit dull.

(b) Motor sailers   An attempt to combine the advantages of power and sail was a natural development in the

A Motor Sailer

growth of cruising and for many the motor sailer may seem the ideal boat. Broader than a sailing boat and with a more powerful engine, the typical motor sailer usually has an enclosed wheelhouse, making a pleasant sun lounge on a cold day, and may have something of the spaciousness of the motor boat in its internal layout — that is, if it is a large and expensive one.

It aims to achieve three things. First, it should give a more comfortable sea passage than the motor boat, because sails have a steadying effect, and together with a keel will reduce the rolling which, in a straight motor boat, can be trying. Secondly, it reduces the danger of being stranded by a mechanical failure or damage to the propeller through floating rubbish or cellophane, because with sails you should always be able to make some port, even if it is not the one for which you were aiming. Thirdly, it makes possible the fun of sailing instead of motoring when the wind is suitable. The sailing performance of these motor sailers is not brilliant; the sail area is smaller than that of a similar-sized yacht, while the windage resulting from the high wheelhouse will act as a brake so that beating into the wind may be impossible. With a head wind therefore the motor will have to come into use, with or without steadying sail according to conditions, but a beam or following wind may give a pleasant day's sail.

Motor sailers, incidentally, can be found with any of the accommodation plans described in Part 4.

(c) Sailing yachts   If you decide that a sailing yacht is what you really want you will be immediately confronted with a number of other technical decisions, each of which will affect your life afloat. The most important of these are

   Draught and type of keel
1.   A deep single (fin) keel, ideally not less than 5 ft, is needed for fast sailing because it gives the boat a better grip on the water and enables it to carry a larger sail area, by providing a counter-balance to the pressure of the wind on the sails. So, for long fast passages you need a deep keel boat. The

disadvantages when trying to creep into a river with a shallow bar have already been mentioned and this type of boat is not suitable if most of your cruising is likely to be in shoal waters.

2. Length of keel is as important as the depth. On a cruise you may want to visit harbours which dry out, and with a fin keel you can only do so by leaning against a quay. If you take the ground without support you will go over so far that living aboard is impossible. Even against a wall, however, you need a long fin keel to settle comfortably and an unsuitable keel will partially restrict your planning of the cruise.

3. A centreboard or drop keel combines the advantages of the deep keel for sailing performance and shallow draught for shoal waters. The difference in depth, for example in our own *Kala Sona*, is 3 ft 6 ins. with the plate up and 5 ft 9 ins. with it down. There are some who say that a centreboard boat always leaks, but we have sailed in one for years without any trouble. When raised, the plate is housed in a casing inside the cabin, which often obstructs the floor space. There are designs with an L-shaped plate which obviate this difficulty, though these are not common and in general this is typical of the sort of compromise decision you have to make. Do you accept some inconvenience in living quarters to obtain the most versatile sailing boat?

With a draught of 3 ft or so a boat can take the ground safely and it will be possible but uncomfortable to live aboard. In order to sit upright you need a boat with a flat bottom, like the old Dutch barges or Shuttlewood's barge-yachts. Many of these do not sail very well, except in sheltered waters, and so modern designers have attempted to combine the advantages of the flat-bottomed boat with sufficient keel to ensure safety at sea and an adequate sailing performance. The result is —

4. Twin or bilge keels with a draught of between 3 and 4 ft. The sailing performance may be a little less good than that of a boat with a single keel, especially when going about, but for many this is outweighed by the convenience of being able to sit upright in a drying harbour, whether or not there is room by the quay, or of exploring and anchoring in shallow creeks where there is no water to lie afloat at low tide.

The type of hull and its effect on sailing characteristics

The dedicated racing man is happiest when sailing 'on his ear' and the masochists who take part in races like the Fastnet may be living at an angle approaching 45° for days on end. When cruising, however, most of us find that this is uncomfortable and tiring, and no fun for anyone except the helmsman. Everything becomes an effort when you cannot move without holding on, or use your hands for the simplest tasks without wedging yourself in.

There is no single-hulled sailing boat which will not heel at all, but the degree of heel and the speed with which the boat reacts to puffs of wind can be modified by design of the hull. The experts will be able to look at a hull and tell at once whether that yacht will be stiff or tender. It depends primarily whether she has a flat turn of the bilges, almost approaching a barge bottom or whether she is a deep keeled V-shape. The former will be stiff initially while the latter will be tender initially. For the beginner the only test may be a trial sail, supplemented if possible by the opinion of other owners of the type of boat concerned.

We have been speaking of the lateral cross section and its effect on the balance of the yacht. There is also the longitudinal outline to be considered. The old straight-stemmed boats had a better grip of the water and would lie to a sea anchor comfortably but they were slow when going about. The modern yacht with its bow and stem overhang, i.e. big difference between length overall and length along the waterline, will spin easily on its central axis, obviously, but will be less stable when lying ahull or running and will probably not lie to a sea anchor. This doesn't matter as nowadays few experts think this a good idea anyway.

Sails and sail plans
The five main types of yachts are:

Yachts with one mast
SLOOP — with mainsail and single foresail
CUTTER — with mainsail and twin foresails

Yachts with two masts
SCHOONER — masts of equal height or the foremast lower than the main mast
KETCH AND YAWL — Main mast is taller than the after or mizzen mast; the placing of the latter determines the difference between ketch and yawl. In a ketch the mizzen is forward of the sternpost and carries a larger

sail. The rig is shown in the drawing of a motor sailer on page 118.

A Bermudan sloop

The two main types of rig, either of which can be used with any of the five types of yachts are:

BERMUDAN — with mainsail raised right to the top of a tall mast

GAFF — with the head of the mainsail attached to a spar (the gaff) which comes out at an angle about two thirds of the way up the mast, leaving a triangle to be filled in by the topsail. This of course is the rig which is seen in all the picturesque old barges.

In addition in the smaller yachts there is a third possible rig:

GUNTER — this rig has a shorter mast with an additional spar which is hauled up like the gaff, but

123

then swung up until it is nearly vertical. It is a useful rig for canal cruising because of the ease with which the mast can be lowered and stowed, but it is only suitable for smaller yachts.

The Gaff rig is now regarded as cumbersome partly because of the weight of the spar, and partly because it is less efficient except when running. So in practice the Bermudan sloop is the most common type of yacht today. The main variation, which is appearing with increasing regularity, is the Bermudan ketch, the theory being that a ketch is easier to handle, particularly with a weak crew, because the sail area of the big mainsail in a sloop can, in a ketch, be divided between main and mizzen. Each sail, being smaller, may therefore require less effort to hoist and lower. This advantage has to be weighed up against the disadvantage of having an extra sail to handle.

Headroom below and the height of the cabin top

In a deep-keeled boat the floor is well below the waterline, giving ample headroom without having to raise the cabin top. The shallow-draught boat, however, is a different matter and in the older boats it was accepted that one of the disadvantages was that the cabin inside was limited to sitting headroom, because any superstructure designed to give more height would have an adverse effect on both appearance and sailing qualities. As E.F. Knight, a celebrated cruising yachtsman of the 1880s and author of the classic *Falcon on the Baltic*, once remarked philosophically, 'If one wishes to assume an erect position one can always go on deck.'

Modern yachtsmen, however, are not so stoical about discomforts and to popularise some of the newer boats,

124

cabin tops have been getting higher and higher until some look like miniature arks.

It is a trend that worries many knowledgeable yachtsmen, because a small boat with too high a superstructure may be unsailable under adverse sea and weather conditions and may even be a death trap in really bad weather. Looking at some in the Boat Show, I could see no possibility of beating out of a semi land-locked bay against a rising on-shore gale.

So, if you insist on the double advantages of a shallow draught boat and, say, 6 ft headroom, you must recognise that you cannot achieve these and a seaworthy boat below a reasonable size. You will not get it in a 24 ft yacht; in this you should be limited to good sitting headroom in the cabin and about 4 ft 9 ins. to 5 ft in the doghouse. At about 27 ft you will get your 6 ft 2 ins. in the doghouse but 5 ft 10 ins. may be a maximum in the cabin and it is only at about 32 ft and more that the tall

A Catamaran

man will be able to stand upright in the main cabin; even at this size he is unlikely to be able to do so in the forecabin.

Single- or Multi-Hull? The Case for the Catamaran

We yachtsmen tend to be a bit conservative and many of us are inclined to regard a multi-hulled boat as a bit of a monstrosity. What is more, we are also inclined to condemn them, without any experience, as boats which at best would give one no satisfaction to sail and at worst may be dangerous, partly because of the stresses weather will produce on the hull structure. We ourselves, indeed, have to admit that although we have enjoyed a good party on a friend's catamaran we have never sailed in one, so have no first-hand experience.

Talking to catamaran owners, however, and particularly those with many previous years' experience in normal yachts, the thing that stands out is the unanimity with which they have been converted to catamarans as ideal boats for a family cruise. Their accommodation has already been discussed in Part 4, though we may not have emphasised sufficiently the value of the spacious foredeck and cockpit as a play area for children. It is, however, the performance at sea that has really excited these new owners. The catamaran is not only a fast boat, but it heels very little and has what one of our friends described as 'astonishing stability'. As he wrote when describing his first year's cruising in the *Cruising Association Bulletin*,

Both at anchor with the wash of passing vessels or the little lop of wind against tide so often encountered, literally nothing slides. The same is true under way at least until sea

conditions become decidedly hostile, and even then it is only
the least stable objects, such as the grill pan, which shift; the
chart has never yet slid off the chart table, and we have
virtually forgotten the meaning of 'passage stow'

Like any other twin-keeled boat a catamaran can take the
ground and remain upright and the draught of many of
them is under 3 ft.

So, why don't we all rush to buy catamarans? I don't
know; there seems to be only one major disadvantage.
Most marinas look at the width and promptly charge
double fees! But, whatever their merits, I cannot help
feeling that it will be a generation or two before the
average cruising yachtsman gives up his normal yacht for
a multi-hulled vessel. Perhaps it has something to do with
my own feeling of delight when at the tiller of a sensitive
single hull, immediately sensitive to any change of wind
strength or direction — it needs a light touch like a good
mouthed horse.

Wood or GRP?
Though the range of materials used in the building of
small boats is widening — the Dutch are using steel and
in Britain there is a vogue for ferro-concrete, usually on a
do-it-yourself basis — for most of us the choice still lies
between wood and GRP, with the latter predominating.
If, like us, you are old-fashioned and want a wooden
boat, it is still possible to find boatyards making them, but
you may have to search.

The wooden boat, even when built to a standard
design, offers more scope for individuality than its plastic
counterpart stamped out of a mould on a mass-
production basis, but, as we shall see when we get to

maintenance, it also demands more care. Wood, if neglected, will rot; GRP may look just as scruffy but will not come to any actual harm unless there are cracks and only the superficial appearance will have to be restored. Moreover, a GRP boat will be lighter than most wooden boats of the same size and is thus more likely to be trailable. This indeed may be the determining factor for many who have space and wish to save money by parking the boat in the back garden when it is not afloat.

The auxiliary engine
Many boats are designed with one particular engine in mind and no other engine, with its associated stern gear, will fit into the available space. In choosing a yacht you may therefore want to consider the choice between:
1.   Inboard or outboard motors and
2.   If inboard, petrol or diesel.

The outboard motor is used mainly on small, light yachts, but among the larger craft it is common on catamarans. One of its attractions is the ease with which the propeller can be cleared if it gets entangled in weed — or cellophane bags — but for obvious reasons it is of very little use in a really rough sea.

A yacht designed for an outboard motor may have no space for one inboard. In the majority, which start with space for an inboard motor, the basic choice is between the petrol engine, which is lighter but consumes more fuel, and the heavier diesel, which is more economical to run, safer, less subject to faults, and requires less maintenance. There is some prejudice against diesel on the grounds of smell, but I think you will find that most yachtsmen, once they have tried a diesel, would not change back to petrol, which requires larger fuel tanks for the same cruising range.

One other point may be worth making here. It is tempting to think that the more powerful the engine the better your speed. This is just not true of boats, whose maximum speed through the water is determined by the shape and length of the hull. It is comforting to have some reserve power to help maintain speed in heavy seas or temporarily against an extra strong tide, but most of the time if you use too much power you will only be pushing up water, instead of increasing the speed of the boat.

Buying a boat

Looking around

Having your own boat built is one of the most exciting things in life, particularly if the boatyard is near enough for you to visit it frequently to watch progress. Even with a standard GRP boat there will be details and alternatives left for you to decide and in some there will be a chance to have a few of your own ideas incorporated, particularly in the internal layout. Before you embark on this excitement, may we sow just two little seedling thoughts in your mind. First, don't be too ambitious if this is your first boat, unless you have already had several years' cruising in other boats. It takes two or three years of living afloat before you know what you really want and it is better to start with a boat that is not too large or expensive. If you want to change later, it is always easier to move into something larger than something smaller.

Secondly, however impatient you are to place your

order, don't be in too much of a hurry as you need plenty of time to look around first. A visit to a Boat Show is valuable and for those near the South Coast there are late summer and autumn shows at Plymouth and Southampton as well as the main show at Earls Court each January. In addition, a great deal can be learnt just by walking round yacht harbours and, if the owners are aboard one that takes your fancy, do not hesitate to ask them what it is. You will be unlucky if they fail to invite you aboard to look round. Visit boatyards too, if they are building one of the types in which you are interested. They will appreciate that you are trying to make an important decision and will do their best to help.

The secondhand market

The pages of the yachting magazines are full of advertisements for secondhand boats and among them you will find some very good buys. The fact that they are on the market does not mean that they are worn out; any boat that has been properly maintained deteriorates very little and the owner may well be selling for the same reason that you will be selling in a few years' time — he is ready for something bigger.

But the layman will seldom be able to judge for himself whether the boat is in good, seaworthy condition. That is an expert job for which you need a survey and you should never buy a secondhand boat without one. If the owner objects, be suspicious; there are plenty of other boats available and the objection may well mean that he has something to hide. This is particularly important if you happen to have fallen for one of the older, wooden boats. Many of these have great character and it is easy to convince yourself that she must be all right, without insisting on a survey. You might even have been taken on a short trial run without discovering that she leaks like a sieve. So, always have a survey and as an extra precaution find your own surveyor —a boatyard should be able to recommend somebody reliable.

Building your own boat
Designers and boatyards are very conscious of the fact that many would-be owners are short of money and they have done all they can to help the do-it-yourself man. Many standard designs are now available at a variety of stages, leaving a proportion of the work to the owner. Cheapest is to buy in kit form at little more than 10 per cent of the price of the completed boat. If you think that will take too long to build, you can buy it as a shell, with only hull and cabin completed or, at little more than half the finished price in sail away condition, complete except for the inside. It will take a great deal of your time, but you will at the end have a new boat at a secondhand price, or less, and you will be able to fit a lot of your own inside furnishings.

The real cost
Comparing prices realistically   We are not going to attempt here to indicate comparative prices for different types of boat, as any figures quoted would probably be out of date before this book is published. What we would emphasise is the care you need to take when comparing prices. Because individual requirements vary, some boat builders prefer to quote a minimum figure for the basic boat, leaving most of the fittings, however essential, for

131

the list of extras. Others take the opposite view and quote a basic figure covering everything you need, even though the individual owner may want to dispense with certain items. In looking at prices, therefore, every list has to be checked in detail to see what it includes and what it omits!

Essential equipment   The main extras on which you may need to spend money include

Sails: The inventory may include no more than a minimum suit of sails — mainsail, foresail and storm foresail. For the first season you might manage with these to see how the boat sails, particularly if you are restricting yourself to coastal cruising. Later, and certainly if you are aiming at long passages, you will want to add:

At least one genoa — a large foresail for light airs
A trysail — a small storm canvas heavy weather sail used instead of the main in near gale conditions.
A No. 2 foresail

Not essential but highly desirable later in life is a dutch-rig boom foresail which obviates sheeting in and winching because it has only one sheet. It is ideal for those friends who wish to practise beating in confined estuaries!

Anchors and chain: Two anchors, (preferably CQR as they have much greater holding power in most bottoms) main and kedge, are a minimum. Some inventories include only one. In many boats, too, only 15 fathoms of anchor chain are provided, and this is not enough. There is one hint here which may save expense. Chain is usually made up in 15-fathom lengths and has to be specially made in any other length. It may be cheaper to buy two 15-fathom shackles of chain and join them rather than have a special 20-fathom length made for you. If you are cruising in rocky areas or where there is a lot of kelp you will need a fisher-man type anchor because your CQR will only ball and drag.

Fenders and Warps: The minimum, we suggest, is six fenders (allowing three for each side if they need protection simultaneously), one bow fender to prevent the anchor chain rubbing and 4 warps — two of these of 14-fathom length (about 26m) and two of 7 (13m).

Navigational equipment will be one of the main items of extra expenditure when buying your first boat. The essentials are:

Ship's Clock and Barometer —and do buy these from a shop specialising in nautical equipment. Both are subject to vibration and to changes of temperature which they would not get at home and need to be specially made to cope with the conditions.

Two compasses — one for steering and the other for use by hand when taking bearings.

Charts, parallel rules, dividers and magnifying glass.

Radio — any transistor radio which will get long wave will do — you may even have a spare one at home.

In addition to these essentials you will need as soon as you start the longer cruises:

Some form of log for measuring distance.

An echo sounder for finding the depth (this you will have acquired very early even if only for anchoring in your home estuary).

Some direction-finding radio for taking compass bearings on radio beams.

Safety equipment: You hope never to need this, but that doesn't absolve the skipper from responsibility for the safety of his crew and he needs:

Two lifebuoys — one fitted with a light.

A personal life jacket for each member of crew.

Flares (red and white) and Very pistol for summoning help.

Safety harnesses which the crew should wear whenever working on deck at sea.

Tools: Again this is a very personal affair but there are a few certain basic musts! The best way of tackling this problem is to list what operations you must take appropriate tools for. Then you can determine whether some are interchangeable.

You need tools for dealing with:

1. All engine maintenance and repairs and this includes not only sets of spanners, screw drivers and gauges but heavy wrenches for seating problems and prop-shaft work.

2. All Electrical Gear. Engine alternator and all regulators and fuses etc. Navigation lights: cabin lights; refrigerator; fans in the heads and radios, if not ship-to-shore transmitter.

3. All gas equipment and sealing for rejointed tubing of gas stoves and lights.

4. All plastic work on a GRP hull or carpentry work on a wooden hull, cabin furniture, dinghy, oars etc. and suitable vices to hold wood and plane it. Also spare

bits of wood for all emergencies including doghouse lights stove in by broaching to.

Work out what you would need in your home workshop for each job and then double any really vital tool — it may fall overboard far from any Friesian Island harbour. Even in England a dockyard matey to do a simple carpentry job is jolly expensive, but abroad you really are on your own, very often, and if you can't even change an injector or bleed your own engine or splice a rope or scarf in a temporary spar repair you will be in trouble.

Winter cover: A large canvas cover made to fit each boat is needed to prevent undue weathering while laid up, unless it is under cover.

Dinghy: Even if you expect to moor exclusively in marinas it is unwise to go to sea without a dinghy —you never know what may happen. Many of the problems of selecting the dinghy were explained in Part 3. A hard dinghy may be either wood or GRP, and maintenance will be similar to that needed for the yacht. The only point we would add here is the need for adequate fendering. At anchor or on a mooring the dinghy, on a wild night, can indulge in maniac behaviour, dancing around at all angles and bashing the boat's topsides. Protective fendering is not easy as we have found nothing on the market that is fully satisfactory. After years of experimenting, the best is home-made. We acquired a length of old fireman's hose (from any fire station) lubricated it with with talcum powder inside and then stuffed it with about ten dozen old tennis balls. This gives

135

you a modicum of flotation as well. To attach it, drill a few holes and just tie it on.

Dinghy outboard motor: You may think you can do without this and row. You may also find that after a long row once or twice against wind and tide you change your mind. Most yachtsmen now regard the outboard as essential. Let's face it, even a superman cannot row four people for a mile against a headwind and a three-knot tide — which is common on the East Coast.

Help with the cost
Marine mortgages Covering about 70 per cent of the value of the boat and repayable over four to five years are obtainable on suitable boats. These must be British registered boats and mortgages will not be given on those at the lower end of the price range, below about £5000. Full insurance is naturally compulsory during the currency of the mortgage. As usual, the names of suitable firms can be obtained from advertisements in the yachting magazines.

Partnership arrangements It is not unusual, either, to halve the cost by sharing the boat with a friend. Evolving a timetable to give each partner a fair share of the season will not be difficult. What tends to be harder is to ensure that both do a fair share of the work, but there is nothing insuperable in such an arrangement, with good will on both sides.

Chartering Hiring your own boat to friends for short periods is often less satisfactory and it is probably better, if you have the right sort of boat, to arrange for a charter firm to make the business arrangements. Many of them are glad of an additional boat or two during the peak period in the summer.

Maintenance

To listen to some yachtsmen talking, one would assume that maintenance is an unending job which leaves little time for actual cruising. We have always found that the time required tends to be exaggerated. The essential annual jobs are:

Fitting out at the beginning of the season

Anti-fouling the hull This, the worst of the jobs, is needed on *all* boats including GRP to discourage the barnacles and other marine growth on the ship's bottom. We are lucky in the cold waters round the British Isles that we do not also have to combat the boring activities of the teredo worm. To achieve anti-fouling the boat has to come out of the water, but if she is not already ashore the normal method is either to lean her against scrubbing posts, which will be found at most boatyards, yacht harbours and at some moorings, or to beach her on a reasonably flat, hard piece of sand or shingle. In either event she will be afloat at high water so you will be able to work only for a proportion of the tide. On scrubbing posts you might, given enough help, manage on one tide; on a beach you will need two because you will have to cant the boat and can only reach one side on each tide unless you have legs, which are useful in many drying-out harbours anyway.

To save time, you probably start cleaning as the water goes down. If there is much growth, garden implements such as a hoe and stiff brush are the most effective. Once clean, the bottom has to be painted with special paint, thick, sticky stuff which is hard work to apply, particularly when for much of the time you will be lying on your back. It is a tough dirty job, but once over, the rest is a piece of cake by comparison. Normally, the anti-fouling does not last the whole season. A boat with a foul bottom will lose a great deal of speed, so those who are meticulous will go through the process again half way through the summer. It is certainly worth doing so if you contemplate a long passage in the autumn; otherwise, I am afraid, many of us shirk this second coat.

Topsides 1. Wooden boats   The purists say that topsides need rubbing down and repainting (even, say some, with two or three coats of paint) every year, and indeed if you have all the time in the world you might like to spend your summer this way. In practice, after two or three years a new wooden boat acquires a thick enough protective coat to enable you to get away with a light rub down, just enough to key in the new paint, and a single coat of new paint is enough unless in the previous season she has suffered much damage. It will depend a little on the type of cruising. Lying against quays or locks is far more destructive to paint than a swinging mooring where the main enemy to the topsides is the dinghy — and that trouble can be eliminated by good fendering. The time taken will depend on the size of the boat, but we reckon that two of us can rub down and paint a 27 ft boat within a day. In any case too many coats are as bad as too few and will merely cake and add weight in the wrong places.

Topsides 2. GRP boats   The theory is that these need so little maintenance. Repainting, for example, need only be done about every six years. But in between repaints keeping the gel coat in good condition entails (a) washing it down and (b) polishing with a good, non-silicone wax polish at least once a year. Experts add that this should be done in spring, summer and autumn and I personally find it difficult to see a great difference in time and effort between painting and polishing.

Brightwork   In most boats, including GRP, there is a varying quantity of varnished wood — bulwarks, handholds, cockpit seats, hatch covers and so on. In a wooden boat the brightwork is likely to include the cabin sides. This, by the end of every season, will inevitably show signs of wear and need rubbing down and re-varnishing with two, and if badly worn three coats. But this part of the fitting out does not have to be finished, like anti-fouling, before going afloat. Even topsides can if necessary be done from the dinghy, though they are easier from the ground, and for the varnishing there is no point in doing it before you are ready to enjoy a good weekend aboard. Nor, does it all have to be finished at once; if a good first coat has been applied, the second and third can be done in idle moments of a later cruise.

Laying up
The amount of work will depend on the arrangements

for winter lay-up. The possibilities are:

1. Afloat in a yacht harbour.
2. In a mud berth, which means being afloat for part of the time. In most mud berths, which are on the saltings, it is necessary to choose spring tides to get the boat in and out. Such berths are cheaper than those in marinas, but you probably cannot spend the odd night aboard.
3. Ashore in a boatyard either in a covered shed or outside under a winter cover.
4. At home in your garden if light enough to trail. The cost of the trailer, which has to be made to fit each individual type of boat, will of course be an additional item in the first year.

If the boat is to stay afloat in a marina there is no need to take the mast down, as in any other type of winter berth. Some owners have their own mast-lowering equipment; others get the boatyard to take the mast out, usually by crane. It tends to be an expensive item in the winter's bill and once you have a boat you expect to keep for several years, it may be worth getting your own simple sheerlegs for lowering and raising the mast to save recurrent expenditure. Once out, the mast must be carefully stored to prevent any danger of bending.

If the boat is coming out of the water for lay-up it is usual to clean the bottom at once. Otherwise there is little to do except to clean up, clear out any gear, particularly electrical, which might be damaged by damp and inhibit the engine.

Insurance

As already mentioned, boat insurance is not compulsory.

In our view it should be, and we would advise all owners both to insure their own boat and its gear for its full value, and also to take out the maximum third party insurance that their company will give. Terms vary considerably and it pays to shop around. It is normal to insure for six months in commission and six months laid up and premiums may be lower if you take out cover for coastal cruising only. Most companies are prepared to make special arrangements for any cruise outside the normal terms of the policy.

Running costs

Again we are not quoting any figures, because so large a proportion of the cost is determined by the biggest variable — the permanent mooring; but the following check-list may help you to ensure that you have not forgotten any major item when working out the cost of running your individual boat in the particular area in which you have chosen to cruise. Some of the items will not be applicable in all circumstances.

1. Permanent mooring or marina berth during the summer.
2. Winter berth whether ashore or afloat.
3. Pulling out of the water and re-launching.
4. Raising and lowering mast and mast storage.
5. Harbour dues — sometimes chargeable in addition to mooring fees.
6. Boatyard labour in laying up and fitting out, in particular fixing ridge pole and winter cover.
7. Material used in fitting out (assuming all work done by owner): anti-fouling, sandpaper, paint (under

141

and top coats), varnish.

8. While cruising, temporary harbour dues and mooring fees in centres other than the home port.

9. Insurance.

10. Yacht club subscription.

It is not, of course, compulsory to join a yacht club, but you will soon find in cruising, both at home and abroad, that many clubs offer facilities which you are only too glad to enjoy — a bar, meals, toilets, wash basins, showers, facilities for washing and drying clothes, telephone and even an address to which post can be forwarded. Though visiting yachtsmen have no right to use a club to which they do not belong, most clubs offer reciprocal hospitality to those based elsewhere. All they ask is that the skipper should go and see the secretary to enquire whether he and his crew may use the club and sign the visitor's book. In most clubs the members will give visitors a warm welcome and there is no charge for the use of facilities. In fairness therefore most yachtsmen feel that they should contribute to the common pool through membership of their local club, even if they expect to use it little themselves.

Apart from these, the only costs when cruising are the obvious ones of food and drink, engine fuel and domestic fuel. The former of course need be no more expensive than at home, the second depends how far you are going and the likely use of the engine (with many diesels using no more than one third of a gallon an hour this cost is negligible) and domestic fuel is much less than the summer electricity bill at home. There is no telephone bill either.

You may at first be startled by the size of the total bill, but if you compare it with the likely cost of any other family holiday you may discover that cruising is the only holiday you can afford.

Part 6

'Going Foreign'

Building up experience by coastal cruising

After the first gentle cruise in sheltered waters most beginners need another year or two before they are ready for foreign cruising, increasing their range gradually as they cruise up and down the coast. To give you some idea of the fun you will be having in the process we might, before crossing the Channel, have a quick look at the cruising possibilities in different parts of the British coast.

East coast — from the Wash to the Thames
Unless you happen to live there, you are unlikely to visit the northern part of this area by sea. The north Norfolk coast is beautiful, but with harbours that dry out for a mile or so and shifting channels it is no place for a small boat which is 'a stranger in these parts', especially in an on-shore wind. Nor do we see much point in going up to Yarmouth or Lowestoft; there is little to do when you get there except to go into the very crowded Broads or turn round and go home. The most northerly harbour which is fun for a cruising yacht is Southwold — that is if you

can get in. The entrance silts up periodically and up-to-date advice is needed on its state since the last gale.

From Aldeburgh southwards, however, this coast has everything for the yachtsman. Don't believe those who tell you that it is dull and flat; its rivers with their little hills and old woodlands, their saltings aglow with the sea lavender and twisting rush-lined creeks that haven't changed since primeval times, have a quiet beauty of their own. Even the mud that spatters your slacks adds to the attraction with its indefinable changing colours, quite apart from its interest as a haunt for wading birds. There are plenty of rivers too. The Alde, the Deben, the Harwich estuary, which we have already visited in Part 3, the Blackwater and Colne, Crouch and Roach and finally the Thames itself with the Medway and the Swale. There are nearly 50 miles here packed with interest and in cruising from one river to another, threading your way between the offshore banks, you will get as much practice in pilotage and buoy spotting as you could wish. Indeed, it is said that Drake was a good seaman primarily because he learnt his trade among the shoals and sandbanks of the East Coast.

This is an area where you will normally spend the night at moorings or anchored, though marinas are beginning to creep up the coast.

South coast — Chichester Harbour to Poole Harbour
You need, we suggest, to gain a little confidence before venturing into the most popular cruising area in Europe. Once you get there, the reasons for its popularity, apart from the easy access from London, will be obvious. There is not only plenty of good, sheltered water, but

there is an extraordinary variety of scenery within this small area. Chichester harbour is backed by the South Downs; the Beaulieu and Lymington rivers wind their way peacefully up into the New Forest, while the Isle of Wight is rightly famous for its cliff scenery, whether you are looking at the north western corner where brilliant, rainbow coloured cliffs give way to the dazzling rugged whiteness of the Needles or at the 'Back of the Wight' with its precipices and chines and caves, once the favourite haunt of smugglers.

As we have already hinted, however, for some of us this area is spoilt by its congestion, necessitating extensive use of marinas and trots to fit all the boats in. On the island there is one beautiful unspoilt creek, Newtown, where you might, on a weekday evening outside the main holiday season, have the luck to find yourself anchored on your own and when you want a change from sophistication you can always go on to Poole harbour, which we mentioned in Part 2.

The West Country — from Exmouth to Plymouth

This again is an area for exploring rivers. The Exe and the Teign may be a bit off-putting because of their difficult entrances but once past Torbay you will be torn between the Dart, and Salcombe river and the Yealm, with spectacular cliff scenery every time you go out to sea and even a possible call into the enchanting River Avon running into Bigbury Bay. All these rivers are near enough together for a nice, easy day's sail as you go from one to the other, after you have finished exploring the beauties of the upper reaches, though that, nowadays, is best done under motor, so congested are these rivers becoming.

As the chart will show, you do not go in too close to admire the cliffs between Start Point and Bolt Head because this area was famous for shipwrecks in the days of sail and the rocks extend well out to sea. Indeed, if a fog comes down you give up trying to sneak into your chosen river and push straight out to sea where, unlike the East Coast, you are free from outlying dangers. In an emergency you should be able to find safety either in Plymouth harbour or round the corner in Torbay.

Cornwall — the South Coast from Looe to Mousehole
From a base in Falmouth described in Part 2 a series of enchanting little harbours extends east and west, but unfortunately in both directions there is a long day's sail before you reach them. To the east, moreover, the fishing harbours of Looe, Polperro and Mevagissey may be dangerous to enter with an onshore wind, leaving Fowey as the only harbour of refuge which you can be certain of getting into whatever the conditions or state of the tide. To the west you have another 30-mile stretch, past the famous Manacles with its collection of wrecks before you reach the area round St Michael's Mount. There is a possible anchorage here and you could have a safe though disturbed night in Newlyn or dry out in Mousehole, but the two long passages do spoil the whole of this Cornish coast as a cruising area.

The Midland and Northern parts of the British Isles
Though I suppose there are more yachts in south coast

Through the Crinan Canal to the Minches and Mountain Lochs of the Western Isles. This is perhaps the most spectacular cruising area of all — but — study the tide rips and watch the willywaughs from side glens and remember to carry a fisherman as well as a plough anchor.

ports, you now have not only equally good facilities but glorious cruising grounds in the North and West of the British Isles, if that is where you live and will want to sail. The only disadvantage is that you are further away from foreign countries, which are always fun to visit for a change now and then. The Pembrokeshire coast deserves to be better known, with its safe harbours like Fishguard and Milford Haven and numerous sandy coves and offshore islands, while in North Wales the Menai Straits and Anglesey offer plenty of scope for short cruises. Though you can't easily 'go foreign' there is good

Taking the Ground — at Barfleur (Normandy). There are a very great number of harbours that dry out and apart from tending warps you will need legs or at least a masthead line to remain upright against the Quay — so be prepared.

cruising to Ireland and the Isle of Man.

Ireland itself offers unlimited scope with its friendly harbours, its deep bays, loughs and isolated coves, with their hilly backgrounds and rocky cliffs. Here you can still find quiet anchorages and see no other yacht for days, but the west coast is exposed to the Atlantic and strong westerly winds will quickly build up a formidable sea.

The west coast of Scotland is regarded by many as paradise and indeed there can be few cruises more fascinating than a potter amongst the Western Isles with their variety of hill shapes and the colour of the glens as

149

the shafts of sun play on them, and the ever changing light on the water as the cloud shadows chase each other across the heather braes. No doubt those who are brought up to sailing in these parts take in their stride the tide rips and overfalls in some of the narrower channels, the strong winds, the mist and rain which can blot out all signs of the only refuge — the rock-strewn entrance to some tiny harbour. For those unused to all this, we would suggest that it is no area for the beginner and it is better to look forward to coming up here later, when it may be just as adventurous as any foreign cruise.

For comfort, most of us would prefer to cross Scotland by the Caledonian Canal than to sail round its north coast and for those living in the east it must be a godsend. It enables one to keep the boat near home in one of several good harbours on that coast and yet to get across easily to the other side for a longer holiday cruise.

Coming back south down the east coast, there is one more cruising area to mention, the Northumbrian coast. It offers miles of gleaming white sands and a number of small attractive harbours where your companions will be picturesque cobles, still being built in the same way as they have been for centuries. In good weather you can cruise among the Farne Islands and you will find few more delightful anchorages anywhere than those in the Coquet Roads, or The Kettle in the Inner Farnes, or, best of all, Holy Island harbour with Lindisfarne Priory on one side and the castle above you on the other.

But the trouble on this coast is that so many of the harbours are too dangerous to enter when the wind is onshore and you cannot hang round near the shore looking for partial shelter — it is far too unfriendly an area with its outlying rocks, shallow water and dangerous seas. If an onshore gale gets up there is nothing for it but to push off out to sea and ride it out, not much fun for a beginner.

This indeed applies the whole way back down to Yarmouth so few of us sail here from choice. Everywhere else round the British Isles an offshore passage will be fun; up the east coast it can be both dreary and exhausting.

Crossing the Channel

The possible routes

For a first passage, most of us will think automatically of the shortest possible crossing from Dover to Calais. And before we even leave Dover, don't forget that the little book Auntie sent for Christmas on 'who gives way to whom' under Rules of the Road, won't have been read by the Ferry skippers! This short crossing is only 22 miles and in fine weather you may not even be out of sight of land, but it has its snags. You may, if the wind is unhelpful, spend most of your holiday merely getting to Dover; by the time you arrive you find that it is time to turn round and go back, without getting across the Channel at all. The other snag is that, quite apart from dodging all the big ships in the narrowest part of the Channel, this is by no means the easiest crossing, owing to the fierce tides round Cap Gris Nez, as many a channel swimmer has found out to his cost. If you can get the tides right you may be across even in a small, slow yacht, in three or four hours. If you get them wrong it could take ten hours or more.

It is not so easy to get the tide right either. At both the

'It says here they've changed the rule about power giving way to sail!'

obvious jumping-off places, Dover and Ramsgate, the outer harbour can sometimes be so uncomfortable, owing to swell, that you are likely to start off with a seasick crew unless you give them a restful night by locking into the inner harbour. But once inside, you cannot get out again until near the next high water and that is about three hours too late for the tide.

So in many ways it is better to try one of the longer crossings. The most popular (and the distances involved in nautical miles) are:

Dover/Dunkirk	38
Dover/Ostend	60

Yarmouth (I.O.W.)/Cherbourg	65
Newhaven/Dieppe	65
Newhaven/Le Havre	87
Harwich/Ostend	79
Harwich/Zeebrugge	79

In most boats, 60–70 miles is not an unreasonable distance for a long day's sail if the wind is favourable and with an early start. If you are off by at latest 4a.m. you should in the middle of summer be across to the other side before dark. In many boats you can contemplate the slightly longer passages of about 80 miles. Most of us find that it is worth this one long day so that we can get to the planned cruising area without delay, but if you want to achieve this you must be single-minded about your objective. You are not setting out for a jolly day's sail, when it does not matter if the wind falls light and your speed drops to a knot or two. You are setting out to cover 60 miles or so in the shortest possible time. If the wind allows you to keep up your speed sailing, you will not only get there but have a delightful day in the process. But, if the wind is not co-operative you should be prepared to help the sails with the motor, or even take them down if necessary. I know there are purists who will disagree about this; it is all a question of what you enjoy. But if you think twelve to fifteen hours at sea is long enough for a young family who need a proper night's sleep then you forget about being a purist.

Setting watches

Everyone is a bit excited at the beginning of a long passage and, if it is the first time out of sight of land, everyone will be slightly nervous too. The skipper will be anxious about keeping the compass course and may not be helped by a navigator who casts surreptitious glances at the compass to see whether he is doing so. Once the land has disappeared the sea looks immense and to your astonishment you find that even in the Channel with its heavy traffic, you may in the wider parts appear to be alone in the ocean. Nobody wants to miss anything so the whole crew stay in the cockpit. The day is broken up by the arrival of food or hot drinks and by watching the other ships which appear from time to time over the horizon. Some hours pass and the skipper starts to feel tired, only to realise that everybody else is asleep in the cockpit. He takes pity on them and soldiers on. By the time some of them are awake the navigator is starting to look for a landfall. It will probably be another hour before anything is visible — one always starts looking much too soon — but it no longer seems worth taking a rest and so it can be a somewhat tired skipper who faces the entrance to a strange harbour.

Normally he gets in safely, even if he is a little short with the crew in the process, but let us just think what happens if something goes wrong at this stage — an adverse wind, an engine which suddenly stops or, worst of all, fog. The harbour may be unattainable and our tired skipper may be faced with several more anxious hours at sea.

Any sea passage in a small boat is a serious job and needs an efficient crew; a tired crew will not be efficient.

The only way to avoid this is to insist on the normal sea routine of watches on any passage likely to take more than about four hours, and those off watch should be persuaded that, for part of the time at least, they should go below and lie down, however little they like the idea. Most important of all is for the skipper to be strong-minded and insist that he has his share of the off watch periods.

Preparing for the passage
Whichever way you are crossing the Channel, you will I hope have done your navigational homework, not only on the course, but also on the tides. Navigating is not easy in a small boat at sea, and for many of us the chart table is not the happiest place to be if we are feeling queasy. Advance preparation is essential to reduce the work you have to do on passage down below and to arrange it in a form that can be taken out into a corner in the cockpit.

The one other important advance preparation is food. Cooking at sea is no easier than navigating and we have never yet found on any passage, up to about 36 hours, that any of our crews wanted to sit down in the cabin to a proper meal. This does not mean that they had no appetite, but they wanted food to eat with their fingers in the cockpit. So, we would try the night before to get things ready and make a series of small packages, stowed in some corner where they could be pulled out easily however much the boat was heeling and being thrown about. Then the only work in the galley would be boiling water for hot drinks. There have been unfortunate occasions when, after spending an evening cutting sandwiches, the forecast next morning was so bad that we didn't go. The sandwiches stayed in their wrappings, as we hoped we would get off the day after. We didn't; so we ate everything up and set off on the third day with nothing prepared! Vicissitudes like this are just part of life when cruising.

The first gentle cruises — the coasts of northern France and Belgium

Once across the Channel there is a choice of delightful harbours to visit, and I expect by now your friends will have warned you not to be too ambitious in your planning, or to start with too many preconceived ideas of the distance you will cover. If you try to do too much, you will only get tired and will not enjoy the holiday. It is important to realise from the outset that you are unlikely to sail every day. You may be held up by weather, you will need the occasional make-do-and-mend day to ensure that the boat and its engine remain in good condition, or you will decide just to stay in port, either because you are tired or because you do not want to tear yourself away from an enchanting harbour. For planning purposes, it is safest to assume that two days out of every week will be spent in harbour.

For gentle pottering you could not do much better than the French and Belgian coasts from Cherbourg along to Breskens, because there are plenty of attractive harbours within easy reach of each other and less outlying dangers than you will find later in Brittany. What is more, you are never far from home. On so many cruises, the need to allow time for the return passage is a bit inhibiting, but along this coast there is no need to retrace your steps unless you want to; you can always get back to some part of the English coast without too long a passage. It may not be your home port, but if time has run out you can leave the boat there and go back for it another week-end.

The only real difficulty, particularly along the Normandy coast, is that many of the harbours dry out, sometimes several hundred yards to seaward and you have to wait for half tide to get in. Furthermore, unless you are lucky, the quays against which you had hoped to dry out are all taken up by the local fishermen by the time you get there. Nor can you rely on settling comfortably on the sand and mud of the outer harbour if you have twin keels, because all the suitable spots are taken up by local moorings and in between, in harbours such as Le Tréport, you will see when the tide goes out that the mud is intersected by the most hideous looking gullies and holes. This does not mean that these harbours will not give you a comfortable night, you can always lock into the Bassin à Flot, but it does mean that your arrival and departure will be restricted by the opening times of the locks, usually about one hour each side of high water. The harbours are just too far apart for you to get out of one as soon as the lock opens and into the next before it closes, so quite a short passage might mean staying at sea for ten hours — an attractive proposition if the weather is right for a good sail or a day's fishing, but not so good if it blows up. Then you must make for one of the bigger ports — Cherbourg, Le Havre or Dieppe — which you can enter at any state of the tide.

With that proviso, however, this coast has much to be enjoyed, so we might assume that we have crossed the Channel to Cherbourg and are sailing east from there to look at some of the highlights. The first, just round the corner is the little fishing harbour of Barfleur. It dries out and you lean against the quay watching the fishermen as they unload an incredible collection of sea monsters — five-foot, shark-like creatures with skins like leopards', and six-foot conger eels, bat-like skate and grotesque miller's thumbs the size of footballs. It is a typical French harbour where nobody is in a hurry, and if you can muster a few words of French you will find the fishermen eager to talk and make a good story of the time they were caught across the Channel, fishing within the limit, and got away with it on a technicality.

Across the Baie de la Seine you have a choice of Courseulles — an attractive little harbour full of reminders of D day and the Normandy landings — Ouistreham and Deauville, where you will find a friendly welcome. If you are short of time, however, you should hurry on to the most picturesque and enchanting harbour we have ever sailed into — Honfleur. The entrance dries out, but once through the lock you lie afloat in the central square of the old town, where nothing much has changed since Henry V was there and the same old medieval houses abut onto the quays. The only difference is that they would not, in the Middle Ages, have thought of lighting up the old gateway.

If, after Honfleur, you should want a bit of variety you can enjoy yourselves by running up the Seine for two or three days. It is a beautiful river with high chalk cliffs and wooded valleys rising above little villages like Caudebec, the famous haunt of painters, with its fifteenth-century church and shady streets and further on, the wonderful seventh-century monastery of Jumièges standing out white in the evening sun. Duclair is a good place to visit but I must warn you that this tidal part of the Seine, where you must certainly work your tides or progress will be very slow, has its snags. You cannot just run into a pleasant village quay as on the rivers and canals we have been telling you about in earlier chapters. The quays not only dry out, but they dry out onto a nasty jagged heap of stones shelving away from the bank. The offshore posts are meant for much bigger river steamers and you will have to leave a duty watch if you tie up to them.

This all means a dinghy, as the only safe thing to do is to anchor in one of the sandy bays or moor to the occasional metal mooring buoy for the night. You will find some of these at most ferry crossings and the locals don't seem to mind, if there is nobody about to ask. If you must see the cathedral of Notre Dame and do some drinking and shopping at Rouen, I advise you not to be long moored to the quay on the starboard side just below the railway bridge — the only feasible place — because there is a lot of traffic and your boat, which must not be left unattended, will in any case get a pounding against the stones. We reckoned this was certainly no place for the night and returned to our mooring buoy by the ferry at Mesnil sous Jumièges where we had another pleasant night.

The entrance to Le Havre is easy and there is plenty of room inside for small boats, but unless you are forced to take refuge there because of the weather you will probably prefer to go on east to one of the smaller ports like Fécamp. Dieppe, which comes next, is useful because you can always get in. The town is more attractive than you would expect and you will enjoy the market with its fish stalls offering succulent varieties to take back and eat aboard. In reasonable weather you can avoid locking in and stay in the outer harbour, but in a swell you will be happier in the Bassin Duquesne.

We have already mentioned the picturesque harbour of Tréport, but we won't linger there because we want to take you next to our favourite haunt along this coast, St Valéry sur Somme.

Don't be put off by the look of the large-scale chart, which is a must. It will show you eight miles of drying out estuary sands, but if you enter two hours before high water and follow the buoys, which are constantly being moved and may include S bends, you should have no trouble. Last time we came out *au clair de la lune* and I don't recommend it. Once in, you will find it difficult to leave the charming old town with its friendly fishermen and good food — the *moules marinières* are superb. Just above the quay there is now a comfortable marina where you can lie afloat.

If the Battle of Flowers is on, or some other fiesta, stop and join in, it's great fun. The country folk from the surrounding villages come in on their floats dressed as Polish dancers, cowboys, stage coach passengers from another age and there will be half a dozen local bands together with sailors and beauty queens and the lot. All the floats are decorated with fresh flowers, to represent butterflies and a range of quite unheard-of beasts. There is folk dancing in the streets, in which everybody is expected to participate. A magnificent Chinese dragon with sixty legs makes a slow and erratic progress down the street at the head of the procession and every few hundred yards it stops. The legs crawl out from under the body, which folds up like a deflated balloon, and the legs disappear into the nearest café to resuscitate themselves. They come out very happy and the dragon reassumes its original shape. The front starts off with a jerk at right angles and rams a peanut van doing a roaring trade at the street corner while the tail collapses in disorder. A gendarme sorts it out, points the indecisive animal down the street and all is well.

Boulogne and Calais will be regarded mainly as staging posts before or after a Channel crossing, though if you should be gale bound, both are pleasant enough towns for a night or so.

And so we move to Dunkirk and the Belgian ports, Nieuport, Ostend, Zeebrugge and Breskens, which will probably give the first taste of foreign cruising to those who sail from the east coast. You will be more comfortable, finding your way in, if you stick to the main channels because it can be very rough crossing the banks, even if there is enough water to do so safely. Of these ports our favourite is Zeebrugge with its great mole and a friendly welcome for yachts on one side of the fishing harbour.

Inland waterways on the Continent

Even the most dedicated sailing man may sometimes feel he would like a change and for unusual holidays it is worth exploring both the French canals and the Dutch inland waterways. In the latter you can also enjoy some sailing as the main canals have lifting bridges and there is no need to lower the mast. In the French canals, on the other hand, you have to regard yourself as a motor boat. We did try one year putting a short mast up and down between bridges, but the crew soon went on strike. So you have to dispose of your mast somehow and, as you can imagine, the ordinary tall mast tied down on deck can be a menace in locks as it will protrude three or four feet at either end. If the canal section is just an incidental part of a long cruise you will have to manage. Otherwise your best course is to enter and leave the canals at the same point, so that you can leave your mast there and pick it up again on your return. The only other possibility is to have a special canal rig with a shorter mast and smaller sails. We have a little gunter mast which has been used on two different boats and it is surprising how well they have sailed with a reasonable breeze. At least it gives you a 'get you home' rig, so that you do not have to risk a Channel crossing with a single engine.

The French canals
In the north, you can enter the system at three points, Calais, St Valéry sur Somme and up the Seine at Rouen, with branch canals leading into Belgium and connecting up with the Dutch and German networks. It will not take long on these canals to discover how important water transport is on the Continent, for these are commercial highways where great barges come thundering past with the little woman at the helm. If they are in a hurry you keep out of the way, always remembering that they are on business! Nemesis, we should add, is no invention as a barge name. But usually both the barge skippers and the authorities are very kind to small British yachts. We pay nothing for the use of these waterways and most of the

bargees are helpful if you have difficulty in tying up in locks. When we first visited these canals, over ten years ago, there were jolly little villages, with their quays and cafés where you could spend the night, but since then much of the network has been enlarged and modernised and now you need to find a disused basin to get away from the barges. It is not that they mind your tying up to them, but they *will* start at 5a.m. One thing which makes St Valéry such an attractive entry point is that the lower half of the Canal de la Somme has escaped modernisation and is still enchanting.

Wherever you enter the system, all routes eventually lead to Paris, where the authorities have provided moorings for small boats in the centre of the city. What better way to do your sightseeing in a great capital, paying only a nominal sum for your accommodation? After Paris, if you have time to go further, things quieten down and you have a choice of routes to take you eventually, if you wish it, to the Mediterranean. With lighter traffic you will find that there is no better way to enjoy a foreign land. The canals take you into the heart of the country, where you tie up at night in little villages. The lock keepers are in no hurry and enjoy a quiet chat, when you have eventually found them in the vegetable garden and persuaded them to work the lock. Now and again, for a change, you will tie up in the middle of a lovely old town such as Reims on the river Marne or Amiens on the Somme and coming down the canal you will get the loveliest view of the spire of Amiens Cathedral, while in the morning the flower market is no more than two minutes walk. It is not a quick way of travelling and if you want to estimate the day's run when planning, you need to look less at the distance than at the number off locks. How long each lock will take it is impossible to say. You might get through in five minutes; you might, when traffic is heavy, find a queue of barges and wait an hour, but even when waiting you will not be bored if you go along and chat to the bargees. They will be friendly as long as they are certain that you are playing fair and not trying to jump the queue. Our only regret was that they were always too shy to invite one aboard. They look so homely with spotless white lace curtains in the wheelhouse and masses of pot plants and the washing hanging along the deck flapping against the inevitable car. One would have loved to have a look down below.

The Dutch inland waterways

For many of us Holland will conjure up pictures of endless canals and windmills, but for the yachtsman, it is more than this; it is also a land of lakes and a great inland sea (the Zuider Zee, now called the Ijsselmeer) and of broken coast line where the sea has burst through leaving behind islands and sandbanks and twisting channels.

In Holland, lying as it does mainly below sea level, the canals are the real highways, older and often more vital than the roads. Like roads, they can range in importance and weight of traffic from motorway to country lane. Not all the latter have lifting bridges, but there are enough of the smaller canals which do have them to enable a small boat to avoid most of the heavy traffic. It is only where a number of canals meet, near Rotterdam, that you have to weave your way cautiously between the monsters.

As we have already indicated, a cruise in the Dutch inland waterway system is not just another canal trip. To avoid a long sea passage we will assume we are entering the system at Flushing, which can be reached by a series of short hops along the Belgian coast. A short stretch of canal from Flushing takes us across the island of Walcheren through the lovely old town of Middelburg to the equally lovely old town of Veere. Here, moored in the old fishing harbour, we are in the first of the inland lakes. It is not, as those who know this corner of Holland will remember, a natural lake. Until recently this was an area of small, isolated islands where the sea used to rush through the gaps, swirling round the sandbanks and nibbling away at the protective dykes. In the floods of 1953 it did more than nibble and the area was devastated. Faced with the prospect of repairing the dykes the Dutch evolved a much more ambitious scheme, to cut off the whole area from the sea by closing the gaps between the islands at the seaward end. Of the three gaps, the southern and northern have now been enclosed and on one sad day the fishermen of Veere sailed out to sea for the last time, as there is no way out at the seaward end through this southern dam. In the north, access is still possible as there is a lock in the Haringvliet Dam. The fisherman's loss is the yachtsman's gain, for the result is that there are stretches of sheltered, tideless water, with steep-to shores and little islands for anchoring.

There are few short cruises offering as much variety as one to the Dutch inland waterways. The sea passage can be any length to suit your individual tastes and it is followed by stretches on canals, interspersed with a little carefree sailing. Leaving the Versemeer by the lock at the eastern end will lead you back into tidal waters, where ahead is a high bridge and at the northern end a gem of a town, Zierikzee. You can still see here what the whole of this area was like before dams were built and if time is running short there is a buoyed channel out to sea and round the Walcheren shore back to Breskens or Zeebrugge before going home. For a longer cruise there is some heavy traffic to contend with for a short distance before slipping off into the northern of these newly enclosed areas. This time there is a lock on the seaward side and the direct run across the North Sea to Harwich is about a hundred miles.

If you still have time to spare, you can go on north to Amsterdam and Ijsselmeer. Once again there will be heavy traffic for short stretches, but once north of Rotterdam the worst is over. The only snag is that on either of the routes from here to Amsterdam there is a delay, unless the mast can be lowered, at an important bridge. One way, it is the bridge carrying the autobahn into Amsterdam, which only opens for an hour or less at around 0600 and the other a railway bridge is even less civilised. Its only opening is at 0100.

If you want to see Amsterdam, a small harbour gives a temporary mooring, but there is too much swell to give a comfortable night and it is better to lock out through the Oranjesluis into the Ijsselmeer. Just through the lock the Durgedam Yacht Club will make you welcome if you wish to stay the night, or you can go on to the Royal Netherlands Yacht Club at Muiden where you moor in the shadow of the old castle.

Now, recent works may have improved the waters of south Holland, but to my way of thinking the effect in the Ijsselmeer is anything but an improvement. The Dutch have a mania for reclaiming land — well, to be fair to them, they have had to or they would not have had much land at all. But whether it is necessary to do as much as they are proposing in the Ijsselmeer is open to question. So long as the encroachments were round the edges, it didn't perhaps matter too much, but it does seem a little strange, when yachting continues to grow in popularity and harbours are over-crowded, to reduce an area of good sailing water at the southern end. It is still worth visiting, if for no other reason than to see its picturesque old towns, but cut off from the sea they have already lost their old purpose in life and I can see them increasingly suffering the fate of being relegated to a tourist attraction.

This is what has happened to Marken, though it is still worth having a quick look at this unique old Zuider Zee wooden fishing village, preserved just as it was built many hundreds of years ago, despite the tourists and the obviously artificial adoption of native costume. Across the Ijsselmeer, you will see this native costume again at Urk, but here it is a different matter. The only active deep-sea fishing community left on the Ijsselmeer, its fleet of great iron ships with their twin beam trawls goes out to sea on Sunday night or Monday morning, returning on Saturday as fast as their 800 h.p. diesels will carry them, and small yachts should get out of their way if they wish to remain afloat. But it is the men who are interesting, wearing their traditional costume from choice as working gear during a week at sea.

Don't think that because the Ijsselmeer is an inland sea you do not need an up-to-date chart. The changes resulting from reclamation make this essential and there are plenty of shallow areas to trap the yachtsman who overlooks the buoys; and remember, once aground there is no tide to float you off again!

Night sailing

After exploring the old towns of Hoorn, Enkhuizen, Medemblik, and Hinderlopen and possibly enjoying a few days in the quiet, pastoral beauty of the Friesian canals, you may feel that the return journey to the south of Holland is a bit tedious and that you might by now be bold enough for the quick way home, straight across the North Sea from Ijmuiden. It involves a passage of about 130 miles to Lowestoft or Harwich, a passage for which you should allow a minimum of 26 hours, if wind and weather behave well.

Night sailing is often spoken of as if it was a bit of a mystery. It is nothing of the kind and in open weather or an area where there are lighted buoys it is easier than by day, because lights will be visible and identifiable from their different patterns of flashes at greater distance than you could identify a similar object in daylight. A channel with unlit buoys is a different matter and should be attempted only by those who know it well and preferably on a clear night. Night sailing is particularly helpful when making a landfall on a coast that has few distinctive features because the big lighthouses will be visible over 20 miles away. The dodge is to time the passage so as to approach the coast before dawn when the lighthouse will guide you in and reach the harbour when there is enough daylight to find your way around.

There should be no difficulty, either, in seeing other

boats at night and there are really only three things to remember. First, make yourself a key of all the lights that you could possibly see and their characteristics, in terms of flashes and frequency. You must be able to identify them when they appear and you won't want to start searching books in the middle of the night. Secondly, remember that though you can see a big ship, it is almost certain that he cannot see you. You will naturally have learnt the different lights which a ship is obliged to carry and will have ensured that your own are satisfactory, but for practical reasons the regulations cannot impose as high a standard on lighting for small yachts as that required by big ships, and anyhow yours may be obscured by the sails. So, keep a good look out and take evasive action in plenty of time. You can draw attention to yourself by shining a torch on a sail but it will not do you much good. The third piece of advice is obvious; you will get much more sleepy by night than by day and a proper system of watches is essential.

On a clear starry night there are a few things more delightful than sitting alone in the cockpit of a sailing yacht, letting her move easily so that you can enjoy your own thoughts as you sail by the 'feel' of the boat and keep an occasional eye on the compass. The only thing that can disrupt this mood, if you are away from any shipping lanes, is the onset of a fishing fleet with flood lights and entirely erratic behaviour.

A few suggestions for longer more ambitious cruises

The Friesian islands — Dutch and German
When the sea broke through the barrier fringe of the

Friesian islands in the thirteenth century to flood the low land including the Zuider Zee and large tracts of the German mainland, it formed the fascinating wilderness of channels and drying-out sand made famous by Erskine Childers in his book *The Riddle of the Sands*. It is a lonely place, and I think that is part of its charm. At low water the sea birds wander about between the avenues of withies across undulating sands as far as the eye can see and at high water you can just sail a shallow draught boat across the watersheds and lie at night in little pockets or creep into small drying-out harbours behind the islands or along the mainland.

The islands stretch for 140 miles along the coast, sometimes eighteen miles offshore and sometimes closing to about five or six miles from the mainland. There are larger harbours like Terschelling, Norderney and Borkum where deep-draught yachts can lie at all states of the tide if you pick your berth carefully and small ones like Oude Schilde, Ameland and Baltrum where you nestle among the local fishing boats.

You can get to the Friesian islands by gentle stages along the Belgian coast and through Holland, as already described. Or you can take a longer sea passage either to Ijmuiden and thence across to Amsterdam and through the Ijsselmeer to the lock in the north-east corner, or to Den Helder further north. If you want an even longer sea passage you can go direct, but whichever way you go, don't venture into this area without the large-scale Dutch or German charts. They are essential, even though expensive.

From the sea, entry to these islands may not be easy as the gaps between them are littered with sandbanks on which the sea breaks dangerously in any onshore wind. Provided you can spot the buoys without coming too close inshore, you may be able to get into Texel, Terschelling and Borkum so long as there is not a full onshore gale, but the other islands should not be attempted in anything above a Force 5. From the mainland you reach them by a series of channels, which twist in at both ends of the islands, and a favourable tide in one spot may be an adverse one only half a mile away. In good weather and with a shallow-draught boat you can even creep along behind the islands following the *watje* (Dutch) or *watt* (German) channels, which are marked by broomsticks. These passages have to be timed so that you reach the watershed about two thirds of the way along each island near high water. If your timing is wrong or you stray from the route you will ground, which is the reason for avoiding this sort of passage on a rough day as you will bump badly on hard sand before getting off again.

This is not an area for the sophisticated. The fun of this cruise lies in the fascination of finding these channels between and behind the islands and the little harbours have less to commend them. Terschelling is the most attractive, though it is apt to get crowded; Borkum is large, comfortable but rather bleak, while Nordeney we find both unattractive and unwelcoming. Further west when you get to Langeoog and Wangerooge, you are really at the back of beyond. What you have to remember is that these harbours are on the sheltered southern side of the islands whereas their more sophisticated attractions, the fashionable watering places, are on the north side where there are miles of sand and the healthy can best enjoy the benefits of a north wind that comes straight down from the Arctic! We went across Borkum on an enchanting little railway to have a look at one of these resorts. It was full of umbrellas and beach shelters, notices and wardens to regiment the bathing and fat ladies in scanty bikinis. We returned thankfully to our small cabin aboard.

Denmark
There is only one way to see the real Denmark: by boat — and preferably a shallow-draught boat. It is not just that the main centres are scattered over three or four larger islands, but in between you have an enchanting world of clear water and insubstantial little green islands that float just beyond the limits of reality. There are small, coy fishing harbours like Nyord By that you can just squeeze into and larger ones like Agersø that have not noticed the medieval way of life is over in the west. In between, you make your way through shallow twisting channels marked by birch brooms. So tortuous are they that it is difficult to see how anyone discovered their existence and you are terribly aware that if you go aground there is no tide to float you off. Funny little islands pop up from nowhere; the echo sounder drops alarmingly and you go slow while the pilot spots a dog leg which you are about to motor straight across. The next buoy has disappeared and an urgent conference is needed before someone discovers it, while the last turn into the harbour would have been unbelievable if the ferry had not gone in to show the way.

After these concentrated bouts of pilotage there are comfortable harbours to leave the boat in while the crew wanders off along cobbled streets into a dream world of colour-washed houses with thatched roofs and hollyhocks climbing up the walls, or a street of cream-coloured stone and the half-timbered houses of an old medieval town. It does not matter whether you choose to sail up the Little Belt, with its fjords and narrow sounds, potter round the central islands south of Fyn or pick your route through the Smaalandsfarvandet and the Bogestrom on your way to Copenhagen. It is all delightful, but I do suggest that you should not miss Copenhagen. It is always fun sailing into a capital city in your own little boat and the yacht harbour in Copenhagen, the Langelinie, a tree-lined circular basin nestling under the castle, is one of the most charming I know. If you want to see her, the famous little Mermaid is only just round the corner too.

If only Denmark was not so far away — some 300 miles from Lowestoft to the western end of the Kiel Canal! For those in a hurry the quickest way is to sail direct either to the Kiel Canal or the River Eider further north. It will mean two or three days at sea and, if the weather blows up, ports of refuge are in short supply. It may be impossible to get in behind the Friesian islands and the Elbe down to Cuxhaven is no place for a small boat with a strong wind against tide. There is fortunately just one funk hole when it is too unpleasant to stay out at sea any longer — Heligoland.

With a little more time, the passage to Denmark can be more fun using any of the alternative routes already discussed across the North Sea and through Holland. There is only one snag. It is no longer possible to get right across the Friesian canals to Delfzyl with a fixed mast;

you have to go out to sea again at the north end of the Ijsselmeer or a little further east and round outside the Friesian islands.

The Channel Islands

The obvious first cruise from the south coast to the Channel Islands is one we would not recommend to the inexperienced. It is an area of rocky shores and dangerous offshore rocks; an area where the tides run fast and the pattern of their movements between the islands is complicated; an area liable to be affected by sudden fogs. Moreover, there is a shortage of good harbours. Alderney has space but is deep and has no protection from a north-east wind, when there is always a danger that boats sheering about on the end of a long chain will create chaos by dragging their anchors. St Peter Port, the main harbour in Guernsey, is still congested despite many recent improvements; while the new harbour in the north of that island is none too easy to enter. Jersey has never had an adequate harbour for the large number of British and French yachts wishing to visit the island and the situation has at last become so desperate that the main harbour, St Helier, has had to be closed to yachts while improvements are made. In good weather there are delightful anchorages off the smaller islands such as Sark and Helm, but in this area you can never be certain of a quiet night and a change of wind may often have you out of bed to pull up the anchor and make an offing.

So if you want to test your powers of pilotage do go and explore the Channel Islands, but don't be deluded into thinking that you are going there for an easy cruise.

Brittany

Where yachtsmen in eastern England will think first of
Holland and Denmark when planning a cruise, those in
the south will gravitate automatically towards Brittany.
To get there a sea passage can be chosen to suit the crew.
Some will go the shortest way, crossing to Cherbourg
and then, timing the Alderney race, down coast to St
Malo. Others will be ambitious, round Ushant at once
and make straight for the south coast of Brittany. Those
who want to make for the south without rounding
Ushant can do so, if they have a boat drawing no more
than four feet, by going to St Malo and crossing Brittany
by canal. This enchanting, peaceful canal was built by
Napoleon to cheat the British and move his troops to the
Channel coast despite the blockade of Brest. It wanders
off into the depths of the country, through delightful old
towns like Dinan, lock gardens ablaze with flowers and
quiet reaches where, if lucky, you may see kingfishers,
dippers and even a golden oriole. Finally, after
meandering through all the locks, you come out into the
Vilaine river in the south-east corner of Brittany, only a
short sail to the Morbihan or the enchanting islands of
Belle Isle and Houat, with their wild flowers and natural
harbours.

It is a part of Brittany that the ordinary tourist will
never see. Nor, indeed, will the normal holidaymaker,
enjoying the seaside resorts, see the things that worry the
yachtsman — the tricky rock-strewn entrances to rivers
and harbours. Once an entrance has been safely
negotiated, it is tempting to linger in one of the
picturesque harbours or delightful rivers, but it is not an
easy coast and no place for the inexperienced.

175

The formalities

Entering a foreign country

We have already in Part 2 explained the importance of
understanding the International Regulations for the
Prevention of Collisions at Sea and the equal importance
of knowing and obeying harbour signals when entering
or leaving port.

On arrival in a foreign country the crew of a yacht is
expected to clear customs, just as they would if entering
in any other way. Occasionally a customs launch may try
to stop you out at sea. In territorial waters you normally
just heave to if requested. If, as once happened to us in
the Ems estuary, there is a gale and thunderstorm in full
swing and the loud hailer says 'Stand still, little English
yacht and say what you have aboard', I expect you will
give them the advice we did. The usual drill, however, is
to announce the need for clearance by flying, at the
starboard cross-trees, the yellow 'Q' flag. Its strict
meaning is 'My ship is healthy and I require practique'
and the same flag will be flown by the QE2 or a
supertanker. Theoretically, you then stay aboard, waiting
for the customs to arrive and in some British ports they
will do so before you have finished tidying up. More
often, abroad, nothing happens. Finally the skipper goes
ashore to find the authorities for himself, taking with him
the passports of every member of the crew and the ship's
papers.

Until recently it was advisable to become a registered
British boat before going abroad and the official ship's
papers are in nearly the same form as those issued to
British boats since Tudor times. Indeed, years ago

Jerboeen's papers were written in a beautiful copperplate hand, but the scribe must have retired because when *Kala Sona* was registered four years later the hand was pedestrian. Recently, registration has become expensive (about £100) and many small boat owners think it is not worth while unless needed to obtain a marine mortgage. To fill the gap the Royal Yachting Association has produced an international card for pleasure navigation obtainable through yacht clubs. It is not compulsory, but it is certainly safer to carry some proof of ownership of the yacht.

Further formalities vary according to country. In France a green card should be issued at the port of entry and produced to the authorities in every other port visited. In Italy the *costituto* fulfils the same purpose, providing proof of official entry into the country. These regulations, however, do change from time to time and it is up to you to discover those currently in force for the countries you wish to visit. When buying duty-free drink, the supplier will arrive with a customs official to ensure that it is sealed, and the seals may not be broken until three miles off shore. All duty-free drink aboard must naturally be declared on entering any other country or on return home.

Flag etiquette

It is normal for every yacht, when abroad, to wear an ensign showing its nationality; this indeed is compulsory when entering a foreign harbour. In Britain the correct flag is the red ensign, unless you happen to belong to a yacht club whose members can apply to the Ministry of Defence for the privilege of wearing a blue ensign, defaced with a special device peculiar to the club concerned. In addition, in foreign countries, a small courtesy ensign of the country concerned should be flown from the starboard crosstrees. The burgee of the owner's club is flown at the mast head but those belonging to more than one club should ensure that the burgee belonging to the club issuing a special ensign is flown with it.

The courtesies

Yachtsmen as a whole are a courteous group. They greet each other when they pass, as countrymen still do in the more remote parts and it is rare to find that they do not go to help a fellow yachtsman who is obviously in trouble. It is really just a question of good manners and of ensuring that neither the crew nor the boat is a nuisance. Living at close quarters in a yacht harbour — and in foreign cruising you will be mainly in yacht harbours — is rather like living in a large block of flats, where blaring radios or unnecessary noise late at night is a nuisance. It is naturally up to every yachtsman too to help to keep the harbour clean by using whatever toilet and rubbish disposal facilities are provided, even if the former are sometimes a little primitive.

When tied up alongside another boat, which has to be crossed to get ashore, it is normal to go round by the foredeck, even if it is more of a scramble, in order to avoid encroaching on their privacy. In the same way, it is important to see that the boats do not damage each other. The fendering of two boats lying alongside is a joint job and it is not enough just to hang out fenders and hope for the best, or to leave everything to the boat that comes in second. And it is usually appreciated if a newcomer is offered help as he comes in. It is not always easy to set ashore with a warp and fend off at the same time if sailing short-handed, or the crew is not too agile, and a friendly offer to take the warp will be accepted gratefully.

Part 7

The Human Element

Now that we have painted a picture—almost a Persian tapestry — of what cruising is really like, and as we both take our leave of you, we hope it will now be easier to sit down and answer the question we posed in the introduction.

Is this going to be a way of life that will suit you and, far more important, your family?

To answer briefly, let me return to the Smiths' little elementary cruise which, I hope, gave you a reasonable idea of both the good and bad aspects of the life. Cruising is not all fun, it means:

Living in cramped quarters, from which you may not be able to escape as you can in a caravan.

Doing without baths, hot water and a few creature comforts.

Putting up with considerable discomfort when sailing in rough weather and on cold nights, or when being seasick or bored.

Learning to fit in with others in a confined space and doing often unpleasant jobs cheerfully.

Living, at least at times, under discipline that you may not always agree with or understand.

Getting cold and wet and feeling frightened — and if anyone tells you that he is never frightened at sea don't listen to him: if he is speaking the truth he is probably a very bad seaman.

Accidents can happen at sea; when they do, they make the headlines, thus exaggerating out of all proportion the possible dangers of going to sea in a small boat. Many of them are the result of carelessness or being over-tired, but even the most careful and competent crew can run into trouble through a piece of bad luck, like hitting a log on a dark night. But accidents of this type are rare and in a gale it is unusual if it is the boat that lets you down. Most standard yachts can take anything the weather can throw at them if properly handled.

But having said that, just think of the 'goodies'. For over half a century now the ordinary men and women of this island have been going to sea in small boats and if we didn't get cold and wet and at times frightened, we would also miss that inner glow after a dusting at sea, the excitement of sailing your own boat into Copenhagen or Stockholm or up the Seine to Paris. We wouldn't even enjoy that first dinner ashore in a strange country so much.

There is really nothing to compare with curlews calling across lonely saltings on Suffolk estuaries, or the evening light on the sea lavender, or the last whisky and ginger ale in the cockpit after an accurate landfall. If you have ever woken up on one of those mornings in a highland anchorage on the west coast when the whole world is breathless, and looked across the still waters of

Yachts in the Old Commercial Harbour at Hoorn. There are many marinas on the Continent but you will generally find more fun, more room and more variety in the old harbours still used by the local fishing and coasting boats — worth a passing look, anyway.

the loch to the wooded shores of birch and pine and green islands floating just beyond the confines of reality as the wind rises and spreads fan shaped across the still water, then surely you will not be wondering any more why there are such rapidly increasing numbers of those who sail. But then you have only got to lie in your warm bunk and listen to the rain and wind pattering on the cabin top, and think, well I needn't move on today we'll enjoy a day 'at home'. This above all the good things in the cruising life, comes to you when you decide, as we do now and then, to potter off into continental canals.

Sunrise — Butley Creek. Now this could be early morning anywhere you happen to be during your next cruise on the East Coast. In fact it is our own home mooring but, to my mind, waking up to this sight sums up all that cruising as a way of life is about.

When all is said and done, where else can you sit at home and float peacefully through great forests and across still lakes, while far away perhaps you can just hear the rest of the world doing battle on the busy highways? Nowhere else today are you so entirely master of your own destiny in an increasingly regulated age. Once round the first few corners you become part of another world, an older world that has grown up imperceptibly and quite naturally out of the colourful past. You will find how quickly it can become for you, even for a few weeks, a way of life rather than just

183

another cruise.

One moves evenly through a world of cows and fishermen and little village pubs. Churches pop up from behind hedgerows like medieval gnomes in enormous hats, and farmyards and village streets open up noiselessly as you potter on between the green banks. At the end of the day when the shadows of the poplar trees reach across the water and you tie up — why, you are still at home, surrounded by familiar books, pictures and personal bric-à-brac. Neither has there been any packing up in the morning nor unpacking at night. The only difference is that the view through the window has changed, as if conjured up by some invisible back projection machine in nature's studio.

Well, to each his own emotional path to ultimate enjoyment, which means in practice the fulfilment of some purpose in life. To many it can come through simple things like rubbing shoulders with the wild life of remote anchorages, where a boat seems to be accepted as part of the scenery whereas even a man walking makes many of the rare birds shy away. I find cruising is, above all, one of the quickest ways for wandering man to get to know himself and to recognise those simple things of eternal value that children are born with and that we older folk can sometimes retain shreds of through middle age. Perhaps much of the fun is simply the opportunity of pitting your wits against an impersonal universe ... you know you can't win!

Short Glossary of Nautical Terms

Note: This glossary is restricted mainly to the terms used in this book. Fuller glossaries for those who need them will be found in many of the more technical books on sailing and cruising.

Aft	Towards the stern; behind
Anti-foul, to	To paint the keel with a special paint to prevent marine growth
Astern	Behind the boat
Bar	A shoal at the mouth of a river or harbour
Beam	The width of the boat at her widest part
Beam wind	A wind blowing roughly at right angles to the direction in which the boat is sailing
Bearing	The direction of an object measured by compass
Beat	To sail into the wind by tacking — i.e. by a zigzag course
Bilge	The space between the floorboards and the ship's bottom

Boom	A spar extending aft from a mast to which the foot of a sail is attached
Bosun's Chair	A seat for hoisting a member of crew up the mast
Bow	The forward part of a boat
Bower anchor	The main anchor
Bunk	A sleeping berth
Buoy	An anchored float of specific shape and colour indicating the position of a hazard (e.g. sand bank, rock or wreck) near the surface of the water
Buoy, mooring	A float attached to a mooring chain
Burgee	A triangular flag flown at the main masthead showing membership of a particular yacht club
Cable	Anchor rope or chain; *or* a measure — 1/10 of a nautical mile
Cast off, to	To release the ropes attaching a boat to a mooring or the shore
Centre-board	A plate that can be lowered through a slot in the hull to increase the draught
Coach roof	A part of the deck raised to give extra headroom
Cockpit	A well in the centre or stern of a boat from which the helmsman steers
Companion way	Entry (often steps) into the cabin from cockpit or deck
Compass	A navigational instrument indicating North and used to determine direction
Course	The direction in which a boat must sail to reach a given point
Courtesy Ensign	A small foreign flag (the maritime ensign of the country concerned), worn at the crosstrees when in that country's waters

CQR	A type of patent anchor shaped like a ploughshare
Crosstrees	Horizontal struts fitted to a mast to hold out the stays
Deviation	A compass error due to the influence of metal in the boat
Dinghy	A small open boat used as a tender to get ashore or aboard when the water is too shallow to allow a boat to lie alongside a quay or hard
Doghouse	A raised roof at the after end of the cabin
Ebb	The falling tide
Ensign	A flag showing nationality, worn at the stern
Fathom	A nautical measurement of six feet — becoming obsolete owing to metrication but still found on many charts
Fender	A pad to protect a ship's sides from rubbing (e.g. against a quay or another boat)
Fiddle	A raised edge on table or stove to prevent things from sliding off
Foot	The bottom edge of a sail
Foresail	A sail set forward of the main mast
Forestay	One of the mast stays leading forward from high up the mast to the bow
Forward	Towards the bow
Frap, to	To secure running rigging to prevent it beating on the mast

Freeboard	The height of a boat's side above the water
Furl	To collect up the sail in a roll or bundle and tie it to its spar
Gaff	The spar to which the upper edge of a four-sided sail is attached
Gale	A wind of from 34–47 miles per hour — forces 8 and 9 on the Beaufort scale
Galley	A boat's kitchen area
Genoa	A large foresail
Gimbals	A device for keeping stove or lamps level whatever the movement of a ship at sea
Go-about	To change tack by turning head into the wind
GRP	Glass reinforced plastic
Gunter rig	A rig with a short mast and an extension spar
Gybe	To change back when running by turning the stern into the wind
Halyard	A rope for hoisting a sail or flag
Hard	A hard strip, natural or artificial, used for landing on a soft shore
Heads	The sea toilet
Headsail	A sail forward of the front mast
Head wind	A wind blowing from the direction in which the boat aims to go
Heel	To incline the boat at an angle from the vertical
Helm	The tiller or wheel used to steer the boat
Horse	A shoal in the middle of a fairway (also technically a bar running across the boat on which a sheet can slide across)

Jib	The foremost headsail
Kedge	A small anchor
Keel	The lowest central timber or moulding on which the whole structure of the boat is built
Ketch	A two-masted yacht
Knot	A measure of speed — 1 knot = 1 nautical mile (6080 feet) per hour
Lee	The side opposite to that on which the wind is blowing
Lee shore	The shore towards which the boat is blown by the wind
Log	Instrument for determining the boat's speed through the water
Log-book	A detailed record of a voyage
Make, to	To rise (of tides)
Make sail	To set the sails
Meets	Posts, usually with distinguishing topmark, which when lined up show the safe passage into a river or harbour
Mizzen mast	The aftermost mast in a two- or three-masted ship
Mooring	A permanent anchorage to which a boat can be attached
Neap tides	Tides occurring half way between new and full moon with the smallest range between high and low water
Overhang	The part of the bow or stern extending beyond the water line

Painter	A rope attached to the bow of the dinghy for towing or tying up
Piton	An iron spike which can be hammered into a bank and used as an attachment for mooring ropes
Port	The left hand side of a ship facing forward
Reach	A point of sailing with the wind roughly at right-angles to the direction of the ship
or	A stretch of a river
Reef	To reduce the sail area by tying or rolling down part of it
Riding light	An all-round light which hung in the forward part of a boat when at anchor at night
Rigging (running)	The movable ropes by which sails are controlled
Rigging (standing)	The fixed ropes supporting mast or spars
Rowlock	A crutch into which the oar fits when rowing
Run	To sail with the wind behind
Saltings	Flat land at sides of rivers, flooded at high tides
Samson	A strong post in the bow to which anchor or mooring ropes are attached
Seacock	A valve in a pipe passing through the hull to prevent seawater getting in
Shackle	A metal U-shaped fitting with a pin through the open end, used for connecting objects (e.g. sail and sheets)

Sheet	A rope attached to the after end of sails, by which they are controlled
Shoal water	Shallow water
Shroud	A stay giving lateral support to a mast
Sloop	A yacht with a single mast
Sound	To measure the depth of the water
Spring tides	The tides with the largest range between high and low water, occurring fortnightly at new and full moon
Stanchion	A support for the guardrails
Starboard	The right hand side of a ship facing forwards
Stay	A mast support
Stern	The after end of a boat
Stiff (boat)	A boat which does not heel easily under sail
Swig	To tighten a rope
Swing	To turn, when at anchor or mooring, with the change of tide
Tabernacle	Deck fitting for the heel of a mast
Tack, to	To sail into the wind in a series of zigzags
Tender	A boat that heels easily under sail
Tiller	A bar attached to the rudder for steering
Topsides	The ship's sides above the water line
Trots	Wooden posts between which boats are moored
Trysail	A tough sail used instead of the main in heavy weather
Under way	Moving through the water
Variation	The difference between true and magnetic north

Warp	A rope
Weather shore	The shore to windward of a ship — therefore, the sheltered shore
Weather side	The side of a boat on to which the wind is blowing
Weigh	To raise the anchor

Appendix B

A Few Useful Names and Addresses

Yachting Magazines
Motor Boat and Yachting (Monthly)
Practical Boat Owner (Monthly)
Yachting Monthly (Monthly)
Yachting World (Monthly)
Yachts and Yachting (Fortnightly)

Chart Agents
Kelvin Hughes, St Clare House, Minories, London EC3N 1DQ
J.D. Potter Ltd., 145 Minories, London EC3N 1NH

Chart Publishers
Imray, Laurie, Norie & Wilson Ltd., Wych House, St Ives, Huntingdon, Cambridgeshire
Stanford Maritime, 12–14 Long Acre, London WC2E 9LP

Yachting Clothes — a few suppliers

Note: Chandlers' shops, usually carrying some clothing will be found in most yachting centres, whether seaside or up-river. The following list is restricted to a few of the main suppliers to help those who have no nearby chandlery.

Equinoxe, Equinoxe House, Lime Street, Bingley, West Yorkshire, BD16 4SP

Helly-Hansen (UK) Ltd., 12 Ronald Close, Kempston, Bedfordshire

Henri-Lloyd Ltd., 390 Manchester Road East, Worsley, Manchester, M28 6WR

Johnson & Sons Ltd., North Quay, Great Yarmouth, Norfolk

Offshore Ltd., Salcombe, S. Devon

Quadrant (Sailing) Ltd., Quadrant House, 250 Kennington Lane, London SE11

Peter Storm Waterproofs Ltd., 14 High Pavement, Nottingham, NG1 1HP

Yacht Chandlers

Thomas Foulkes, Lansdowne Road, Leytonstone, London E11 3HB

The London Yacht Centre, 13 Artillery Lane, Bishopsgate, London E1 7LP

Capt. O.M. Watts, 45 Albemarle Street, Piccadilly, London W1X 4B7

Bibliography

General
Note: Some of the books in this section also include chapters on navigation, meteorology and maintenance.

Reed's Nautical Almanac (published annually) Thomas Reed
Brackenbury, Mark, *Begin Cruising under Sail*, Elliot Right Way Books
Brandon, Robin, *The Good Crewman*, Adlard Coles Ltd.
Heaton, Peter, *Sailing*, Penguin Books Ltd.
Heaton, Peter, *Cruising*, Penguin Books Ltd.
Heaton, Peter, *Cruising: Sail or Power*, Kaye and Ward Ltd.
Heaton, Peter, *Motor Yachting and Boating*, Penguin Books Ltd.
Hiscock, Eric, *Cruising Under Sail*, Oxford University Press Ltd.
Marriott, Hugh, *Owning a Boat*, Nautical Publishing Co. Ltd.
Nicholson, Ian, *Guide to Boat Buying*, Adlard Coles Ltd.
Pike, Dag, *Motorsailers*, Stanford Maritime Ltd.
Sex, Tim, *Coastwise Cruising*, Nautical Publishing Co. Ltd.
Sleightholme, J.D., *This is Sailboat Cruising*, Nautical Publishing Co. Ltd.
Sleightholme, J.D., *This is Sailing*, Nautical Publishing Co. Ltd.

Sleightholme, Joyce, *The Sea Wife's Handbook*, Angus & Robertson Ltd.

Navigation and Meteorology

Blewitt, M., *Celestial Navigation for Yachtsmen*, Yachting World — Iliffe Books

Blewitt, M., *Navigation for Yachtsmen*, Yachting World — Iliffe Books

Dixon, Conrad, *Basic Astro-Navigation*, Adlard Coles

Gibson, Charles, *Be Your Own Weatherman*, Arco Publications

Rantzen, Lt. Com. M.J., *Little Ship Navigation*, Barrie & Jenkins Ltd.

Rantzen, Lt. Com. M.J., *Coastal Navigation Wrinkles*, Adlard Coles Ltd.

Rantzen, Lt. Com. M.J., *Little Ship Meteorology*, Barrie & Jenkins Ltd.

Reeve-Fowkes, Michael, *Stanford's Tidal Atlas* (2 vols — *English Channel East* and *English Channel West*), Stanford Maritime Ltd.

Smith, David, *Simple Navigation by the Sun*, Thomas Reed Publications

Watts, Alan, *Instant Wind Forecasting*, Peter Davies Ltd.

Whitaker, S.F., *Night Sailing*, Stanford Ltd.

Williams, Capt. T.J., *Coastal Navigation*, Thomas Reed Publications

Maintenance

Blandford, P.W., *Practical Boatman*, Stanley Paul & Co. Ltd.

Jones, Charles, *Boat Maintenance: Ideas and Practice*, Nautical Publishing Co. Ltd.

Jones, Charles, *Glass Fibre Yachts*, Nautical Publishing Co. Ltd.

Du Plessis, Hugo, *Fibreglass Boats*, Adlard Coles Ltd.

Sleightholme, J.D., *Fitting Out*, Adlard Coles Ltd.

Toghill, Jeff, *The Boat Owner's Maintenance Manual*, David & Charles Ltd.

Wiley, Jack, *Fibreglass Kit Boats*, Patrick Stevens Ltd.

Engines

Cox, Tom, *Power for Yachts*, Stanford Maritime Ltd.

Watson, Ted, *Handling Small Boats under Power*, Adlard Coles Ltd.

PILOT BOOKS AND HARBOUR GUIDES

Cruising Association Handbook. The only harbour guide that includes instructions for all harbours normally used by yachtsmen in the British Isles and nearby foreign coasts from Biscay to Denmark. Obtainable from the Cruising Association, Ivory House, St Katharine Dock, London, E1 9AT and on sale to non-members.

British Isles (in geographical order)

Getting Afloat: an annual directory of launching sites in the British Isles, Link House Publications Ltd.

Royal Northumberland Yacht Club — *Sailing Directions, Bridlington to Fife Ness*

Coote, Jack, *East Coast Rivers*, Yachting Monthly

Pilot's Guide to the Thames Estuary, Imray, Laurie, Norie & Wilson Ltd.

Campbell, Capt. F.S., *Stanford's Harbour Guides: River Medway to the Swale*, Stanford Maritime Ltd.

Campbell, Capt. F.S., *Stanford's Harbour Guides, North Foreland to the Needles*, Stanford Maritime Ltd.

Adlard Coles, K., *The Shell Pilot to the South Coast Harbours*, Faber & Faber Ltd.

Adlard Coles, K., *Creeks and Harbours of the Solent*, Edward Arnold

Campbell, Capt. F.S., *Stanford's Harbour Guides, Christchurch to Mousehole*, Stanford Maritime Ltd.

Pooley, D.J., *West Country Rivers*, Yachting Monthly

Glazebrook, H., *Anglesey and North Wales Pilot*, Yachting Monthly

Irish Cruising Club — *Sailing Directions for the South and West Coasts of Ireland*

Irish Cruising Club — *Sailing Directions for the East and North Coasts of Ireland*

Clyde Cruising Club — *Sailing Directions for the West Coast of Scotland*

The Yacht Harbour Guide, National Yacht Harbour Association.

Warring, R.H. and C.W., *Marina Yearbook*, Kenneth Mason Ltd.

British Inland Waterways

Nicholson's Guide to the Thames, Robert Nicholson Publications

The Thames Book, a Link House Group Annual.

The Broads Book, a Link House Group Annual.

The Canals Book, a Link House Group Annual.

South Coast of England, Channel Isles and North French Coast

Adlard Coles, K., *Channel Harbours and Anchorages*, Edward Arnold Ltd.

Robson, Malcolm, *Channel Islands Pilot*, Nautical Publishing Co. Ltd.

Delmer-Morgan, E., *Normandy Harbours and Pilotage*, Adlard Coles Ltd.

France

Guide Renault — Marine des Ports de France, Blondel la Rougery, Paris

Benest, E.E., *Inland Waterways of France*, Imray, Laurie, Norie & Wilson Ltd.

Bristow, Philip, *Through the French Canals*, Nautical Publishing Co. Ltd.

Adlard Coles, K., *North Brittany Harbours and Anchorages*, Adlard Coles Ltd.

Adlard Coles, K., *Biscay Harbours and Anchorages* (2 vols), Adlard Coles Ltd.

Brandon, Robin *South of France Pilot*, Imray, Laurie, Norie & Wilson Ltd.

Bristow, Philip, *French Mediterranean Harbours*, Nautical Publishing Co. Ltd.

North France, Belgium and Holland

Delmer Morgan, E., *North Sea Harbours and Pilotage, Calais to Den Helder*, Adlard Coles Ltd.

Belgium

Benest, E.E., *Inland Waterways of Belgium*, Imray, Laurie Norie & Wilson Ltd.

Holland

Benest, E.E., *Inland Waterways of Holland* (3 vols), Imray, Laurie, Norie & Wilson Ltd.

Bristow, Philip, *Through the Dutch Canals*, Nautical Publishing Co. Ltd.

Oliver, John, *Holiday Cruising in the Netherlands*, David & Charles Ltd.

Germany

Bristow, Philip, *Through the German Waterways*, Nautical Publishing Co. Ltd.

Accounts of Cruises

Note: In addition to books on cruises in specific areas it is worth mentioning the annual collection of logs covering varying areas and published under the title *Roving Commissions*, edited by Alastair Garrett, R.C.C. Press

Pilkington, Roger, *Small Boat through France, Belgium, Holland, etc.*, Macmillan Ltd. (A series of books on cruises in European waterways)

English Canals

Gagg, John, *Canals in Camera*, Ian Allan Ltd.

Doerflinger, Frederic, *Slow Boat through Pennine Waters*, Allan Wingate Ltd.

Liley, John, *Journeys of the Swan*, Allen & Unwin Ltd.

INDEX

201